naughty
or nice
sex

exciting games
and
romantic play
for lovers

amy scott & boyd geary

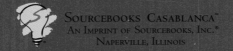
SOURCEBOOKS CASABLANCA™
AN IMPRINT OF SOURCEBOOKS, INC.®
NAPERVILLE, ILLINOIS

Published by Sourcebooks, Inc.
P.O. Box 4410, Naperville, Illinois   60567-4410
(630) 961-3900
FAX: (630) 961-2168
www.sourcebooks.com

Originally published in 2002

ISBN-13: 978-1-4022-0577-4
ISBN-10: 1-4022-5077-5

Printed and bound in the United States of America.
CPI   10 9 8 7 6 5 4 3 2 1

dedication

To my husband, Fred

—Amy

In loving memory of Betty Maloy

—Boyd

contents

acknowledgments

Most of all, I want to thank my parents for nurturing my interest in writing and for believing in me in non-writing matters as well. To my sisters, thank you for the many hours of creative play that helped us all develop a healthy imagination. I also appreciate the encouragement of my literary friends Lisa, D.L., and Cindy. For the inspiration behind many of my romantic notions, I owe a debt of gratitude to the grande dames of gothic novels Phyllis A. Whitney and Victoria Holt, for their tales of reluctant heroines and brooding men having chance encounters in mysterious seaside mansions.

—Amy

I would like to thank my family, especially my mom and sister for always listening to my inane ramblings and for helping me weather more than a few cases of writer's block. Much appreciation goes out to all of my friends. Particular thanks to Martina for inspiring the naughty, Maria for encouraging the nice, and the Divas for blurring the line between the two. And finally, a round of applause to the loonies at work who put up with my endless trivial knowledge of Hollywood's romantic comedies on a daily basis.

—Boyd

A special thank you to Deborah Werksman at Sourcebooks, Inc., who saw potential in this concept and was willing to work with us to make this into something special.

Introduction

So what's it going to be tonight? Something tame, or something wild? A moment that will sparkle, or are you out to create sparks? Whatever your tastes or comfort levels, *Naughty or Nice Sex* has an activity to match your mood.

This book was written for lovers everywhere, for different seasons, locations, lengths of time, and budgets. Some activities are low-key, while others are over-the-top. Add your own personal touches to make them fit your mood, your time frame, and your wardrobe. You can feel confident the nice activities will cause no blushes, while the others...well, you are naughty, aren't you?

Nice

Nature Lovers

Getting close to the earth reenergizes and revitalizes you. Spend a day together beautifying your corner of the world.

❤ Visit a nursery or garden shop and pick out lush green plants for your yard, garden, window box, or for indoor decoration. Or do a fun art project together: stencil a border of ivy leaves on your kitchen or bathroom walls.

❤ If your yard needs a little or a lot of work, do some homework and design a new landscape. Tackle the whole yard or just one section. Or, play farmer for the day by planting an herb or vegetable garden. Spend the weeks ahead nurturing it together, and you will soon be enjoying the fruits of your labors!

❤ For an experience away from home, visit a botanical garden, flower show, greenhouse or nursery, garden show, or butterfly farm to learn more about the natural world, or just for the sheer beauty of it. Be sure to stop and smell the roses!

Naughty

Down and Dirty

Birds do it, bees do it. Feeling earthy? Let nature take its course as you explore the ancient elements of fire, water, wind, and earth.

♥ Create a romantic getaway by surrounding your patio or bedroom with flowers and plants. Spread a tarp on the floor and meet wearing only gardening aprons and gloves. Run your hands over each other with the textured fingers, giving each other a sensual massage. Next, rub each other down with fresh soil, breathing in its rich aroma. Now, spray your mate with a misting bottle of water to create an invigorating mud pack. Then take it to the mat with a mud-wrestling match.

♥ When you're done, fill the bathtub and sprinkle the water with essential oils. Swirl in rose petals to create an aromatherapy experience as you bathe together. Light incense and let the gentle breeze of a fan waft its fragrance over you.

Nice

You're the Top

Top ten lists have become staples of popular magazines and late-night television talk shows. Why not take a break from hectic "to do" lists and create a list both you and your mate can enjoy?

❤ Schedule an afternoon to spend together compiling a list of reasons that you first fell in love. Take your time and reminisce about the blossoming of your relationship. From the ideas you create, choose the ten that mean the most to both of you. Make two copies of the final list to keep in a purse or wallet. Having these shared memories is sure to bring a smile to your face even when you're not together.

❤ Partners can become so wrapped up in their daily routines, they forget to take time out for the little things that make a relationship so special. Create a list of ten activities you would like to enjoy as a couple. Post your list where it will be seen each day. Choose a time to put the grocery list aside and set off on an adventure together.

The Hot List

Have you ever made love on the beach at sunset? How about necking in the back of a theater during a movie? Well, now's your chance!

❤ With your mate, put together a list of ten romantic ideas that you have always wanted to share. Throw caution to the wind and choose daring locations or racy experiences in the privacy of your own home. Using just a little imagination is sure to spice up your love life.

❤ For a fun variation, make a list of sexy situations involving your mate. Ideas like "I want to kiss every inch of your body" are sure to get your mate's attention. Create a note card for each idea, slip it into an envelope, and seal it.

❤ By candlelight, ask your mate to choose one of the ideas and read it aloud. The anticipation of knowing what lies ahead will only enhance the experience. Work your way through as many of the ideas as you wish. Chances are, your partner will have a few ideas, too!

Nice

Free Time

If the best things in life are free, then you can have a great time without spending a lot of money! It just takes a little thought and a quick scan of your local newspaper. What activities can you find that are free or dirt cheap? Organize an entire day of things to do that don't cost a cent.

- ❤ Visit a public park or garden, attend the grand opening of a store, cheer on runners in a marathon, attend a free seminar at a home improvement store, listen to a lecture at your library or hospital, volunteer to help a local organization for the day, attend an open house, wander through an art gallery, visit a hotel and have a drink in the lobby bar, sit in the cheap seats at a sporting event, go to a garage sale or flea market, or head for the library and pick out books you've always wanted to read.

- ❤ For an economical lunch, have a picnic somewhere along your travels, eat at a fast-food restaurant, use a two-for-one coupon at a restaurant, or pig out on free samples at the grocery store.

Naughty

Cheap Date

Do bad boys and girls have all the fun? Find out by taking a walk on the wild side and acting out your naughty date fantasies within the safety of your relationship.

❤ For a stay-at-home experience, make your bedroom the "red light district" by putting red light bulbs in the lamps, getting fringed lamp shades, and spraying cheap perfume around the room. Chill some cheap wine or beer and drink it out of paper cups. Surprise your mate by wearing your sleaziest bedroom attire.

❤ If you're going out, find a dimly lit restaurant-bar and sit in a booth. You'll have your own private corner for snuggling, playing footsies, and seeing where you hands will travel when they're under the table. Tell your partner you're not wearing underwear. Kiss passionately every time the waiter leaves.

❤ Then go to a dance club with sexy, pulsing music that brings out your primal instincts—and your body heat. Dress in your tightest clothes and dance so close people will think you're glued together.

Nice

Money's No Object
When was the last time you and your partner were able to enjoy a little luxury? Can't remember? Well, reach up, grab that brass ring, and enjoy the ride!

❤ Spend some time together relishing the fruits of your labor. Realizing that not everyone has been featured on *Lifestyles of the Rich and Famous*, make plans that won't land you too far in debt.

❤ Share an evening together exploring a new dining experience or order an expensive entrée at a favorite eatery. Schedule a romantic evening dinner cruise and watch the moonlight hand in hand.

❤ Plan an evening on the town and rent a limousine. Dress up and spend an evening at the theater, stopping off for a nightcap or coffee to end the evening.

❤ If you would rather stay in, order take-out and serve it on your best china. Splurge on an expensive bottle of champagne to complete the meal. However you choose to be extravagant, do it with style.

Naughty

Indecent Indulgence
There are no greater riches than love, but pampering yourself and your mate never hurts!

❤ Go all out to create a seductive experience that the two of you will talk about for months. Plan a weekend getaway to a nearby luxury resort. Many hotels offer packages that include continental breakfast. Selecting a sexy new negligee or silk boxer shorts for the trip is sure to make sightseeing much more enjoyable. If you ever leave the room is up to you.

❤ How about bringing a piece of paradise home? Go shopping together for a new bed. Nothing says romance quite like a large four-poster bed. Outfit your new purchase with feather pillows, satin sheets, and a large, fluffy down comforter. You may have to give the bed a trial run before deciding to keep it.

❤ Start a new post-lovemaking ritual by feeding each other delicacies like chocolate and strawberries. Share a nice bottle of sparkling wine together in bed. Soon you'll be creating your own champagne kisses and caviar dreams.

Nice

A Fragrant Reminder

Our sense of smell is hardly noticed in our day-to-day lives, yet fragrances are a large part of how we define ourselves. How many types of scented products do you use—from shampoo to car air freshener?

- ❤ Make a potpourri of the fragrances that make up your partner's "scent profile" for a take-with-you reminder of his/her special aroma.

- ❤ Collect tiny samples of the items that scent your mate: drops of cologne (put them on a small square of cardboard or fabric), a sliver of soap, shavings from a candle, a dab of hair products, a few granules of laundry detergent, a spritz from an air freshener, and even a pinch of favorite herbs. Stir them up and capture them in a piece of lace tied with a ribbon.

- ❤ Make one for yourself of your mate's fragrances and one for your partner of your fragrances. Carry them with you all week, in your car, purse, or briefcase. Every time you need a sense of your partner's closeness, take out the sachet bundle and breathe in those familiar scents. It will seem as if your mate is right there with you.

Animal Instincts

Some foods and aromas have legendary status as aphrodisiacs, or substances that arouse sexual desire. They range from the ordinary, like garlic, to the exotic, like powdered rhino horn. What would happen if you tried them all in one night?

- Have a meal of these potent foods: oysters, caviar, lobster, passion fruit, truffles, wine, sturgeon, champagne, *foie gras* (goose liver), onions, pine nuts, quince, walnuts, grapes, and, of course, green M&M candies. Researchers have found that the smells of baking cinnamon buns, pizza, and roast beef are very stimulating, as are the aromas of chocolate, vanilla, strawberry, and cinnamon.
- What to wear? The most stimulating attire is leather and fur because of the faint traces of their animal origins.
- For a scent-sational boost to your basic instinct of smell, use cologne featuring real or synthetic civet or musk oil, which is taken from the glands of a type of wild cat, or ambergris, which comes from whales. These ideas will increase your animal magnetism and make you irresistible to each other.

Nice

Elementary, My Dear

Does an Agatha Christie novel send shivers of excitement up your spine? Have you ever dreamed of joining Sherlock Holmes on a chase through the foggy streets of London? Perhaps it's time that you and your partner unravel a mystery together.

❤ Plot an adventurous outing for you and your mate. In secret, coordinate all the details for the excursion. Then, several days before your time together, begin to leave mysterious clues for your partner to find. Cryptic riddles or objects that lend themselves to your activity should intrigue your mate. Make sure the clues are ambiguous, so as not to reveal the surprise.

❤ Mystery dinner shows are a fun way to spend an evening together playing detective. Check your area for historic hotels or railways that may offer one of these interactive experiences. An alternative is to host your own mystery dinner party. Kits can be purchased that include instructions for creating a successful night of suspense. Whatever your choice, here's a helpful hint: keep your eye on the butler!

Naughty

Sexy Sleuthing

A mysterious crime of passion is about to be committed in a shadowy house lit only by candlelight. The clues point to only one conclusion: mischief! Whodunit? Only you and your mate can answer that question.

- Creating an evening sure to mystify your mate will take some planning, but it will be well worthwhile. Devise a series of clues to lead your mate throughout the house. Include handwritten notes of encouragement, small sexy gifts, or risqué photos for your mate to collect.

- At the end of the trail, hide an article of your mate's intimate apparel with a note instructing that the item be worn into the bedroom where the suspect is believed to be hiding. Wait in the darkened bedroom wearing only a trench coat. Congratulate your amateur inspector on the cunning it took to solve your perfect crime. And don't be surprised if your mate insists on a strip search!

Nice

Playing Tourist

Are we there yet? Take a mini-vacation without the long car trip by being tourists in your own town, just the two of you.

❤ Plan a day with your partner as though seeing your town for the first time. Get books from the state or local tourism office, collect brochures from a hotel, and combine that with what you already know. Play tourist in your town or one nearby that you've always been curious about.

❤ There's plenty to do: take a long walk in a park, shop in some trendy boutiques, eat in a restaurant, see a museum, attend a festival, or go to the top of the tallest building in town. Are there factory or brewery tours? Wouldn't a horse-drawn carriage ride or water cruise be romantic?

❤ Get around town in ways different from your normal routine, like walking or taking a cab or city bus. Be sure to stay until after dark, when the lights of a town give it a romantic glow. At the end of the day, settle in at a bed-and-breakfast inn.

Naughty

Let Me Show You Around

When you've finished your day of touring, have a night of exploring by giving your mate a guided tour of a very private place.

♥ Grab some body crayons that are available at bath, novelty, or party stores and draw a map on yourself based on your own natural terrain, including roads, points of interest, and natural landmarks. Label these map features using names you and your partner have already assigned them, or think up names suggested by the parts. Twin Peaks and the Eiffel Tower come to mind. Make it a surprise by stripping down unexpectedly and showing your partner "the world."

♥ Get a distance-measuring pen and run it over your mate's body to see exactly how far it is from point A to point B. The shortest distance between two points may be a straight line, but the curves are a lot more fun!

Nice

Capture the Memory

Photographs are a great way of commemorating special events like birthdays, anniversaries, and vacations. Unfortunately, these images often end up in a shoebox buried in the back of a closet.

- ❤ Organizing these precious pieces of your history can make for a fun afternoon with your mate. Start by sorting photos in categories such as holidays and vacations. Purchase photo albums with self-sticking pages or photo boxes to make the task a little less daunting.

- ❤ Take time to remember the details of the events in the pictures. Adding captions and pieces of memorabilia can add interest to your scrapbook. You and your mate may want to use extra photos to create small albums for family and friends.

- ❤ When your scrapbooks are complete, host a party and ask guests to bring their own albums to share. Some companies offer home parties with memory-making ideas and products. Encourage guests to create new memories by providing them with disposable cameras.

Naughty

Sensual Snippets

Looking for the perfect place for that photo of your scantily clad mate or of the two of you in a passionate embrace? Why not create an intimate scrapbook filled with romantic reminders of your time together?

❤ Mix photos of you and your mate on special occasions with more personal pictures you may have captured. The album is only for you and your partner, so don't hesitate to use those racy images.

❤ Also include items that conjure up memories of erotic times together. A matchbook from a cheap motel where you spent the weekend making love or a garter from a sexy Halloween costume are perfect additions. Use familiar pet names and terms of endearment when labeling the photos. Flipping through your scrapbook can be a source of comfort on those occasions when you must spend time away from your mate.

❤ Remember to include enough blank pages for future amorous adventures!

Nice

Fashion Show

Clothes make the man—and the woman. Does your wardrobe need updating, maybe one season or the whole thing? Work on it together, starting with a boost to your fashion IQ.

- Attend a fashion show at a local store, mall, or convention center and scan fashion magazines, taking note of what you like. Then go shopping and pick out clothes for the other to try on. What does your mate pick out that you wouldn't? Does your partner see you as sexier than you do?
- When you get home, model what you've bought, using the hall for your runway. Do all the moves you've seen the supermodels do as your partner does the commentary.
- For an afternoon of self-improvement fun, give each other a makeover or go to a salon together to try out a new hairstyle, pedicure, manicure, or facial. Be sure to offer encouragement when you've tried something new!
- For fun on a date, dress in matching outfits, such as the same color shirt and slacks.

haute couture

Avant Garde

Do you run past Frederick's of Hollywood or charge boldly in? Have a little fun by going shopping for some mood-setting apparel.

- ❤ Go shopping for sexy lingerie and indulge in a lace teddy or silk boxer shorts. Perhaps you're daring enough to try edible candy underwear. At home, have a racy fashion show modeling your new lingerie, going from the least to the most revealing item. Or have a fashion show of sexywear that you already own, with one new piece thrown in to see if your partner is paying attention. For a sexy, clingy look, spray yourself down with water before going "on stage."
- ❤ After the show, have a wine and cheese social, where the model (you) meets the press (your mate). Wear your sexiest lingerie item. It will be a great conversation starter.
- ❤ For some quick fun after work sometime, undress your partner and then dress him/her in an outfit of your choice. See how far you get!

Nice

Box Office Bonanza

There may be no more traditional date than that of dinner and a movie. Heading to your local movie theater is a perfect activity when planning time together is difficult. Although traditional, going to the movies doesn't need to be dull.

💜 If you have trouble choosing a film to see, why not make it a double feature? You and your mate can each pick a film to see and spend the day together at the movies. Don't skimp on the popcorn!

💜 Many areas offer alternatives to modern multi-theater complexes. Cinema and draft houses allow you to share a beer or glass of wine with your mate while watching the latest releases. Small art-house theaters can also be a great way to catch an independent or foreign film.

💜 If you and your mate are avid moviegoers, plan a trip to a metropolitan area during a film festival. In addition to seeing cutting-edge cinema, you can explore the city. Because of the popularity of these events, be sure to plan your trip well in advance and purchase tickets for the screenings you wish to see.

Naughty

Reel Steamy

Have you ever daydreamed that you and your mate are stars of the silver screen involved in a romantic encounter? Share your dreams and make them reality.

❤ Plan a leisurely evening snuggled together in bed watching movies. Choose several sensually themed videos to get your romantic ideas flowing. Share a bottle of wine and talk about the erotic images of the film. You'll be making your own magic before the credits roll.

❤ Take your mate on a getaway to a location featured in one of your favorite romantic films. Reserve a room at the Grand Hotel on Mackinac Island in Michigan and relive the passion of *Somewhere in Time*. Use *An Affair to Remember* as your inspiration and pledge your love for one another on top of the Empire State Building in New York.

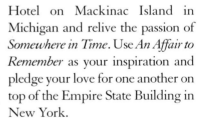

❤ If you would rather create your own sensual film, use a video camera to capture a romantic interlude that you and your mate have planned together. Lights, camera, action!

Nice

Dance Marathon

In the 1950s, energetic couples competed in dance marathons, where they would dance for days on end to win prizes. How long do you think you can dance without stopping? Write down your best guess, then put on your favorite up-tempo music, and dance until you drop. See who gives up first.

💜 Record the songs onto CD in advance so you won't lose your momentum. Use your favorite fast songs from many different styles of music that you like, such as pop, hip-hop, country, and Broadway musicals.

💜 If one of you isn't a dancer, get an instructional video on a kind of dance you would both be willing to try and have fun learning the moves together. Then make your debut at a nightclub that features your new talent.

💜 Or spend the evening seeing how many dance clubs you can visit that feature different styles of music and dancing. Give them all a try!

cutting a rug

Naughty

Dirty Dancing

What music brings out your animal instincts? Is it sultry R&B, suggestive pop, a rhythmic classical piece like Ravel's "Bolero," sensual New Age instrumental, or pulsing urban?

❤ For an outrageous evening, buy your mate sexy underwear and hang it on the bedroom doorknob with a note that says, "Put this on before opening the door." When your mate opens the door, be sitting on the edge of the bed in a sleazy nightclub outfit, with sexy music on pause. When the door opens, start the music and the cheering. Get the dollar bills ready. Then take a turn as the dancer, grab a broomstick, and do the home version of a pole dance.

❤ For a quieter evening, wear outfits themed to the time period that the music is from and decorate the room in keeping with the theme as well. If you're dancing to contemporary music, decorate the room like a dance club: low lights, loud music, and drinks set up on a bar. Start your romantic interlude with a dance.

Nice

Trading Places

Feeling stuck in your normal routine? Take some time out with your mate to experience a change of scenery. Whether it's a short afternoon trip or a weekend getaway, a little change may be all you need!

❤ Fast-paced urban life can be stressful. Map a course and set out on a rural escape with your partner. Explore a produce stand, an auction, or an old covered bridge. Prepare a large basket of picnic necessities and spend the afternoon in a bright meadow or beside a small brook.

❤ If the slow pace of the country is getting you down, make a break for the big city. Visit the hottest tourist spots or spend the day browsing through funky boutiques. Catch a movie or theater production and have a late dinner at a sidewalk café. A ride in a hansom cab is a romantic way to end your evening.

Naughty

Sexy Switch

Is your love life becoming too predictable? Maybe a fresh perspective will mix things up a bit. Remember, all work and no play makes for a very dull love life!

♥ Bid the country farewell for awhile and head to the nearest metropolitan area. Treat yourself and your mate to a sensual massage at an upscale spa, or attend a seminar on human sexuality at the local university. Secretly caress each other as you tour the city by taxicab. Check into a chic hotel, order room service, and put the "Do Not Disturb" sign on the door.

♥ Hectic city living can also take a toll on your romance. Rejuvenate your sex life with an excursion to the country. Stay with friends or family on a farm. Steal away with your mate to the hayloft for a long afternoon of lovemaking. Find a secluded creek and let the cool water wash over your naked bodies.

Nice

Movie Premiere

Celebrities get dressed to the nines for movie premieres. Women wear lavish gowns designed just for them and borrow some of the most expensive jewelry in the world.

- ❤ Have your own movie premiere at home, with you and your mate as the stars. Leave work early to get your hair spruced up, then get dressed up in a fancy dress or tux, and do your makeup and accessories Hollywood-style. Pose together for a picture if you have a camera with a timer, or take your picture in a mirror.

- ❤ Settle down on the couch for the premiere. When the movie's over, set up light snacks on the kitchen table and do your Tinseltown talk—critique the actors, compare the stars' performances to their past work, and discuss the blockbuster potential of the flick. At the end, toast the film and its stars.

Naughty

The Casting Couch

Behind the scenes of the movie industry is not so glamorous. Competition is so fierce for acting jobs that even established actors have to audition, and many a tale has been told of actresses winning parts by paying a visit to the "casting couch," or sleeping with someone influential who's involved with the movie.

💜 Clear the living room couch for the audition. Men should wear tight pants and a shirt open to the waist with gold neckchains, in best sleazy Hollywood director style. Women, you'll need your best come-hither outfit of a short, tight skirt, a braless skimpy top, and high heels.

💜 Enter the room through a nearby door carrying your favorite steamy novel, with the best page marked. Read it passionately to the director, who will need a lot of convincing that you should get the part.

Nice

Role Reversal
Doesn't it always seem more fun to help clean a friend's apartment than it does to clean your own place? Even the most boring household chores can be fun if you don't have to do them all the time.

- ♥ Make a list of chores you and your mate normally do, then switch your lists. Include all kinds of things: picking out a birthday card, taking out the garbage, grocery shopping, and getting the oil changed in the car. For one week, do as many of your mate's chores as possible. Pick some easy ones and some hard ones. You may need to ask your partner for help or do some research. You'll each gain a better appreciation for what the other one does.
- ♥ At the end of the week, share your thoughts about what it was like to experience what the other does. Be sure to tell each other how much you appreciate what you both do.

House Call

Plumbers charge so much that it would be nice to get a little extra service.

💜 Change into a satin robe and arrange some racy undergarments on the bed, where they are sure to catch your mate's eye.

💜 Have your mate arrive in answer to your call about a broken bathtub faucet. Answer the door all flustered; you thought it would be an hour before help arrived. Show your mate to the bathroom through the bedroom. Pretend to be shocked at the underclothes when you see them on the bed and quickly toss them aside.

💜 As you bend over the tub to point out the leak, have your bathrobe fall open. Act embarrassed, yet surprised at the passion it arouses in both of you. Lead your mate into the bedroom.

Nice

On the Fitness Trail

You know that taking care of your body is important, but doing it alone often takes the fun out of the experience. Plan a time with your mate to kick off a new healthy routine.

♥ Start the morning by taking a new class together. Kickboxing, step aerobics, or spinning can get your heart pumping and energize you for the rest of the day. If classes aren't available, locate a nearby trail and go running, biking, or in-line skating. Many old railways are being converted into beautiful fitness paths.

♥ Grab a light lunch of crisp salad or healthy sandwiches and head over to a day spa for an afternoon of pampering. Spas often offer areas where couples can relax together. Have a skin treatment, seaweed wrap, or deep-tissue massage. Then share some time in the whirlpool or sauna.

♥ At the end of the day, your body, soul, and mate will thank you.

Night Spa

Why pay for time at a spa when you can create one at home?

- Set the mood by lighting candles throughout the house. Intimate music and lush aromas will also help create a soothing atmosphere.
- Assemble all the ingredients for your magic night beforehand. Make sure to have massage oils, lotions, and bath salts available. A bottle of wine, fruits, and cheeses complement the evening perfectly.
- Take a long steamy bubble bath together. Dry each other, lingering over each other's skin. Wrap your mate in a big, thirsty robe or bath towel. Give each other long massages with heated oil. A facial complete with cucumber eye presses is a nice touch.
- After spending time in a steamy bath, the touch of cool cotton sheets guarantees a night you won't soon forget.

Nice

Ride 'Em, Cowboy

The wild west has long held a mystique of adventure and romance. Many of us grew up watching images of hard-riding cowpokes and tough-talking saloon women on television and movie screens. Choose a day to get in touch with the cowboy (or girl) within.

- ❤ Greet the day before sunrise and begin your adventure with a big, hearty breakfast. Throw on your dungarees and head out to the country. Go to a rodeo, or try horseback riding.
- ❤ Spend the afternoon browsing through a country-western store. Outfit yourself and your mate in the latest in western wear, complete with boots and hats. Grab some vittles at a local roadhouse and then two-step your way to a honky-tonk for some line dancing. Stay out until the cows come home!

Naughty

Lookin' for Love

The fun of playing cowboy isn't reserved for children. Treat your mate to some playtime, grown-up style.

❤ Clear a space in the living room for a dance floor. Dim the lights and play soft, slow country music. Serve frosty longnecks from a tub full of ice.

❤ Make it a night of adventure as you meet your partner at the door wearing a cowboy hat, boots, and a smile. After some romantic dancing, spread a blanket out on the floor to share.

❤ Any good ranch hand knows the importance of a lasso. With

your partner's permission, use silk scarves or neckties to gently bind your mate's wrists. What happens next is up to you. It will come as no surprise whose bed your boots will be under!

Nice

Be a Kid Again

For many people, life's routine leaves very little time for play. As children, weekends and summertime were a perfect time for playing all day. Take some time out with your mate to rediscover the fun of playing games.

❤ Pick an afternoon and collect some of your favorite childhood games. Some games are more fun as a group, so invite family or friends to join you. Spend the day playing cards, checkers, or even a marathon game of Monopoly.

❤ Set up several tables so that you can play different games at the same time. Serve childhood favorites such as french fries, hot dogs, and hamburgers.

❤ If weather permits, why not venture out into the yard for a game of badminton, croquet, or tag? A big pitcher of lemonade would be perfect for the afternoon. Before you know it, you'll be laughing together and forgetting all about your normal routine.

Naughty

Check Mate
How could marbles or dominoes ever be sexy? Give them an adult twist!

💜 Plan an evening of game-playing for you and your mate. There are several options for selecting games for this special evening. Choosing them together can be half the fun.

💜 Novelty stores often carry adult games that are fun to play as a couple. In addition to getting to know each other better, they can offer some steamy situations.

💜 Many games from your childhood can be given a romantic update. Twister seems much more adult when played in silky lingerie. Other games are already perfect for the occasion. A light-hearted game of kissing tag, spin the bottle, or post office can be a fun way to start a passionate evening.

💜 If all else fails, there is always strip poker!

Nice

Your Creative Spirit
Absorbing yourself in the beauty of the art world will nourish your soul as well as your creative spirit.

❤ Put on your most bohemian clothes, like vests and berets. If you don't have the right threads to make you feel artistic, visit a thrift shop and pick up a pair of funky slacks or a fringed jacket that you normally wouldn't wear. It's freeing to get a little crazy!

❤ Now that you're feeling artsy, go to a museum or an art exhibit. You might also want to attend an art auction. At these venues, try to figure out what you like about the works, and then talk with each other about your preferences. Learning what your mate likes will help you understand each other better.

❤ Afterwards, have a picnic lunch in a park. Feast on wine, cheese, French bread, and grapes. Or go more exotic and have stuffed grape leaves, taboule (finely chopped parsley and tomatoes), hummus (garbanzo bean spread), and pita bread.

Body Art

They say life's a canvas and we're free to paint on it what we like. Take that to the extreme, with a hot one-on-one art session at home.

- ❤ Pick up some body paints at a novelty shop or get colored soap crayons or bath foam at the grocery store. Indulge your fantasies by decorating your mate (or yourself, as a surprise) with colorful creations of your own design. Paint a heart with both of your initials in it.

- ❤ Slowly run the paintbrushes, or your fingers, around each other's curves. You can even press a piece of paper to one of the designs, peel it off, and keep it as a souvenir. Or do several and have your own private art exhibit.

- ❤ If you're truly daring, pretend you're an artist's model. Stand on a stool or stepladder in the middle of the room, drop your robe, and stand naked while your mate, who's pretending to be an art student, sketches you.

Nice

Pocket Change Challenge

In the early '80s, video games were all the rage. Everyone was getting Pac Man fever and scrambling for the latest and greatest game system. Revisit the days when a quarter was all you needed to escape your cares for awhile.

❤ Treat your mate to an afternoon playing games at a nearby arcade. Many malls, movie theaters, and pizza joints feature electronic games. Stick to two-player games and enjoy the thrill of saving the universe together.

❤ Visit a local electronics store and pick out a computer game you can play as a couple. Choose a game that has puzzles and challenges that require you to put your heads together to solve a mystery.

❤ Break out your old game system that has been collecting dust since high school. Spend the evening reminiscing as you challenge each other to classic video games.

arcade amore

Naughty

Erotic Electronics

Is your mate a big kid when it comes to video games? Do you feel like you're battling a game for your lover's attention? You know what they say: if you can't beat them, then join them!

💜 Plan a night to play video games together at home. Challenge your mate for a sexy grand prize by competing for the highest score. Dress in something racy and do your best to distract your partner. Hey, no one said you had to play fair.

💜 Play your favorite video game, but make it decidedly more adult. Strip video games, anyone? For every game you win, your opponent must remove an article of clothing.

💜 Choose an adult title from the local video store. Several games offer characters competing in naughty situations. Add to the stakes by playing in bed. You'll give the term *joystick* a whole new meaning!

Nice

Letter of the Day
Who knew the alphabet could be such fun?

💜 Create a list of fun activities, each beginning with a different letter of the alphabet (A is for archery, B is for bowling, etc.). Randomly pick from the list and set off for a day of adventure not found in grammar books.

💜 Maybe your mate has a favorite letter of the alphabet. Plan an afternoon themed to that letter. Keep in mind xylophones and zebras are scarce in some areas!

💜 To make the day complete from A to Z, start your morning off with a big bowl of alphabet cereal or serve alphabet soup for dinner.

💜 End the day together with a challenging crossword puzzle or game of Scrabble. After such a full day, you and your mate will both be ready for some ZZZs!

Naughty

Lessons in Love
Arithmetic may leave you cold, but the alphabet is sure to have you hot under the collar!

💜 Engage in a racy game of "show and tell" with your partner. On slips of paper, write an article of clothing for each letter of the alphabet. You may have to be creative for some of the more obscure letters.

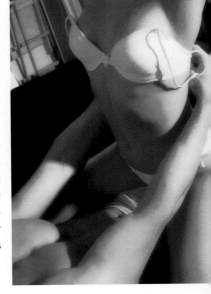

💜 Place all the pieces of paper into a hat and draw them out one at a time. If you are wearing the article of clothing drawn, you must remove it. Take turns between you and your mate. Winner takes all!

💜 Why not create your own special book of love? In a notebook, dedicate each page to a letter of the alphabet. Choose a romantic location to make love that begins with each letter and fill the page with your steamy experiences. Beats algebra any day!

Nice

State Fair
Celebrate the change of seasons by attending a local carnival, fair, or festival.

❤ Once you're there, ride your favorite rides from childhood, like the haunted house, the Zipper, the Tilt-A-Whirl, or the ones you love as an adult. Have your mate play those tricky games of chance and try to win you the most ridiculous stuffed animal prize.

❤ Stuff yourself on classic carnival foods: hot dogs, sausages, french fries, cotton candy, peanut-studded caramel apples, red candy apples, funnel cakes, hot chocolate, and other specialties.

❤ Attend an evening concert at the fair and slow dance under the stars. If it's hot, hold a cold can of soft drink or beer against your mate's neck, or cool each other off by rubbing each other with ice cubes or dumping a cup of cold water over your partner's head!

❤ If you decide to head out of town for your county or state fair, stay in a vintage motel and eat at a diner.

tunnel of love

Naughty

Fun House
Carnival rides are fast, exciting, and sometimes scary, offering lots of opportunities for hugging and snuggling.

- ❤ While you're zipping to the heady heights of the Ferris wheel, plunging into the scary darkness of the haunted house, or floating in the romantic quiet of the tunnel of love, make out as though you're alone for the first time.
- ❤ Fairs often feature side show acts who have special talents. What are your special talents in bed? Work up a couple's act of contortionist moves, then put on leotards and try them out. Lubricating jellies and oils will reduce friction.
- ❤ Livestock judging is part of every county fair. What qualities make for a prize-winning animal? What physical attributes do you look for in a person, and how well does your partner measure up? With a blue ribbon handy, size up your partner by calling out all of his/her notably sexy characteristics. Remember, the judge has to feel the specimen to properly evaluate it.

Nice

Roughing It

After a week of long office hours, bumper-to-bumper commutes, and household chores, some time in the great outdoors may be just what you and your mate need.

- ❤ Put together your backpacks and pull on your hiking boots! Set off on a trip to a nearby state park or favorite hiking trail. If you plan on being out for the entire day, make sure to pack snacks, a first aid kit, and plenty of water.
- ❤ Turn your hike into a photo safari. Pack disposable cameras for you and your mate and capture images of the local flora and fauna. Collect fallen leaves to later identify and use in a memory book of your adventure.
- ❤ Want to make a weekend of it? Pack a tent and enough supplies for several days. Many parks offer reasonably priced campsites. Set up camp and enjoy a few days of hiking, swimming, or just relaxing around the campfire.

Naughty

Nature Lovers

Turn your love loose and go wild! Infuse the romance between you and your mate with a breath of fresh air. Yes, camping can be sexy.

- Whether your idea of camping is sleeping beneath the stars in the wilderness or in a tent in your own backyard, a little creative thinking will have your mate howling at the moon.

- Make s'mores over the campfire and feed each other while they are still warm. Seductively lick the sweet marshmallow and chocolate concoction from your partner's fingers. When your temperatures have risen, go skinny-dipping to cool off. Splash around and let the feeling of the water against your skin send a shiver through your body.

- When it's time to retire for the evening, realize that you have conveniently forgotten to pack your sleeping bag. You'll have to share with your mate. Be prepared to discover the real meaning of wildlife!

Nice

This Moment in Time

Did you know there really is a Tara, a plantation home that was the model for Scarlett O'Hara's mansion? Wouldn't it be fabulous to replay the famous scene between Humphrey Bogart and Ingrid Bergman at the airstrip in Casablanca, Morocco?

❤ Pick out an historic place in your town or one nearby. It may be a significant home, such as the governor's mansion, or a more humble log cabin, a fort, or an old courthouse or jail. Or travel to another state, to a city of historical importance, like Washington, D.C.; Yosemite National Park; Boston; Williamsburg, Virginia; St. Augustine, Florida; or one of many Civil War battlefields.

❤ When you're there, imagine what it would have been like to live then. If you're staying overnight, take along some clothing that reminds you of that time period. Go to a restaurant that serves food authentic to the region. To further surround yourself in the experience, get a book from that era and read it to each other, or rent a romantic movie set in that time period, such as *Gone with the Wind* or *Casablanca*.

Living a Romance Novel

What would it be like to live in another time period? Escape from the concerns of the modern world by spending a weekend immersing yourselves in the past.

- ❤ Stay at a nearby or out-of-state bed-and-breakfast inn that has historical significance—and romantic four-poster beds with curtains. Meet in a meadow or on the fog-laden dock and then steel away for a forbidden tryst.

- ❤ Bring along your most Victorian-looking nightwear, such as a lacy nightgown, a hooded cape, a full-sleeved, open-necked white cotton shirt, velvet or leather trousers, and boots. In the evening, make love by candlelight or firelight, then sip wine together. Read parts of a gothic romance novel to each other—but only the seductive scenes.

- ❤ Or visit a dude ranch out West and learn about its rugged past. Spend the day riding horses along the dusty trail. At nightfall, go for a ride, then stop in a secluded spot and make love on a wool blanket under the stars. Be sure to take along a bottle of tequila.

Nice

Rise and Shine

Setting the alarm a few hours earlier can open a whole new world of possibility for you and your mate. Spend some time together before the day gets too busy.

- ❤ When was the last time you watched a sunrise? Get up early and go for a walk along a favorite trail, or find a place to park and watch the sun make its way over the horizon.
- ❤ Surprise your mate with breakfast in bed, complete with fresh juice, pancakes, and fruits. Take a few extra minutes to lounge beneath the covers.
- ❤ If you and your partner are naturally early birds, why not take over a newspaper route? Deliver the papers together while singing along to favorite oldies or catching up on conversation.
- ❤ Take a break from the rat race and visit a local coffee or doughnut shop. Read to each other from the morning newspaper or watch people as they hurry to work.

Sunny Side Up

Having trouble getting your motor running in the morning? Add a little devilish flair to get things moving!

❤ Get ready for the day by taking an invigorating shower for two. Have a supply of sensual shampoos and body scrubs on hand, as well as natural sponges and washcloths. Linger over your mate's body as you towel each other dry with big, thirsty cotton towels.

❤ Set the alarm for just before dawn. Pull back the curtains and open all the bedroom windows. Throw off the bed linens and make love as the sun fills the room with light. The neighbors will be talking for weeks!

❤ Spend the morning lounging in your sexiest bathrobe. Serve mimosas with the morning newspaper on the deck or patio. Get your mate's attention by offering a seductive peek beneath your robe. Soon you'll be making headlines!

Nice

A Quiet Interlude

Do you have the same old lunch routine: grab something quick in the cafeteria and eat with coworkers, if you even stop to eat at all? Meet your honey instead and you'll both have a wonderful day.

❤ Make a date to get together for lunch during the workday at either your favorite lunch restaurant or one you like that you haven't shared with your mate. If there's a quaint little restaurant that's known as a romantic hideaway, go there. Plan ahead or do it on the spur of the moment, sending a page or email to let your partner know you'll be stopping by or where to meet you.

❤ Arrange ahead of time to have flowers, candy, or a special greeting card delivered to your partner during the meal. If you're on a bigger budget, book a singing telegram messenger to bring a message of love, perhaps dressed as Cupid or a clown.

❤ If lunch time is too busy, make the same plans for after work. Try to make this a weekly or monthly way to freshen your relationship.

lunch date

Naughty

Lunchtime Rendezvous

The clandestine, passionate lunchtime love affair is exciting, and it doesn't have to happen only in the movies. Add this spark to your relationship and make it your own little secret!

💜 You already have the ideal hotel in mind, so check your partner's calendar and make a reservation. If your mate likes surprises, announce it with a page or phone call, telling your partner to meet you in a limo in front of the workplace. Or you can let your mate know ahead of time so you can both pack your favorite sexy loungewear.

Another option is to have your partner meet you in the hotel lobby or bar, and then check in as the Smiths.

💜 Be sure to bring your favorite aphrodisiac foods, or splurge and call for room service. Also bring plenty of candles or incense, bubble bath and a loofah, and be sure to get a room with a big bathtub.

💜 You can also put this plan into action at home by dropping enticing hints about why your partner should meet you there.

Nice

Shaken Not Stirred

The classic cocktail party, evoking images of 1950s men and women talking and sipping martinis, is making a comeback. Plan your own after-work gathering with your partner.

- ❤ Invite friends and coworkers that both you and your mate enjoy spending time with. Set up a bar with several drink options, including nonalcoholic alternatives. Serve light hors d'oeuvres and set the mood with some big band or jazz recordings. Arrange furniture into small groupings that lend themselves to conversation.

- ❤ Looking for something a bit more intimate? Meet your mate at a local hotel bar or cocktail lounge after work. Choose a venue that offers a selection of specialty martinis or features a favorite piano player or lounge singer.

- ❤ Take a bartending class together and learn how to make everything from a Harvey Wallbanger to a Shirley Temple.

Naughty

Make Mine Dirty

Treat your mate to an erotic evening that would make even the Rat Pack blush!

- ♥ Greet your partner at the door with a favorite cocktail or martini. Dress provocatively in a lace teddy or silk boxers and open satin robe. Allow your mate to relax on the sofa while you provide a sensual foot massage. Work the tension out of your partner's weary legs with your hands.

- ♥ Ask your mate to slip into something a little more comfortable while you prepare some finger foods to nibble on. Fix yourself and your mate another cocktail. Put on some Frank Sinatra or Dean Martin and lower the lights for dancing.

- ♥ Make love right there on the living room sofa. Speak in hushed tones and feed your mate olives from your martini. Complete your evening with rich coffee on the patio. If you like, share a premium cigar. The working class never had it so good!

Nice

Night Owls

If opposites do attract, then chances are one of you is a night owl and the other an early bird. See how the other half lives by having the early bird stay up late.

💜 So what do night owls do? Snuggle up on the couch and watch late-night TV shows or movies, or just read together. Maybe you'll want to make your favorite snack. You can also play card games, board games, or video games together, and do some Internet surfing.

💜 Go out for a late dinner, see a midnight movie, go dancing at an all-night club, call friends and family members who are in earlier time zones, or head for a twenty-four-hour store or restaurant and see what goes on when one of you is usually asleep.

💜 For a late-night nature approach, head outside to look for bats, owls, and other creatures of the night. Or drive out into the country and lie on a blanket gazing at the stars. Many science centers have late-night viewing of the heavens through their telescopes.

Naughty

On Moonlight Bay

Nighttime is the right time for being romantic: a full moon, a quiet house, and just the two of you. A full moon has been known to make people get a little crazy. What are your fantasies?

❤ Warm up by renting a racy video or watching a TV or pay-per-view movie that has an adult theme. If you're really daring, videotape the two of you in a romantic situation and play it back. It will probably call for a real-life replay.

❤ Put on your sexiest outfit and go to a dance club that plays suggestive music, and bump and grind among the other club-goers.

❤ If you're back before midnight, have your own special, sexy countdown to that magical hour. Participate in a special warm-up activity every fifteen minutes before midnight, then start the new day in a big way by making love right as the clock strikes twelve.

Nice

Prime Time

Studies have shown that people spend many hours in front of the TV each day. Why not spend some of that time snuggled up next to the one you love?

❤ As a change from regular programming, tune into a cable network that broadcasts classic television shows. Reminisce with your mate about your favorite childhood programs. Or choose special interest channels, like the History Channel, and watch together. Take turns and discuss the programs you see.

❤ Remember when staying up to watch Johnny Carson was a big deal? Well, Carson may have left *The Tonight Show*, but late night television is alive and well. *Saturday Night Live* is another popular choice.

❤ Stay home from work with your mate and watch soap operas all afternoon. You're sure to get caught up in the stories of love, betrayal, and amnesia. Laugh at the crazy lives of the guests on those trashy daytime talk shows.

Naughty

The Boob Tube

Television—sexy? Sure, and so are fuzzy slippers and hair curlers!

❤ Get a little racy in the flickering light of the television set. While watching your favorite program, make a rule that you may only fool around during commercials. You'll only have a couple of minutes to get your mate's blood pressure up. Before long, your partner will be channel-surfing *looking* for commercials.

❤ Play a variation of the "Hi, Bob!" drinking game that has been popular with college students. When a character in an episode of *The Bob Newhart Show* says, "Hi, Bob!" remove an article of clothing. Or make up a new version of this game with your favorite sitcom. You and your mate will be naked before you know it.

❤ Turn down the volume and turn up the fun. Watch television with the volume off and create your own dialogue. Invent sexy back-stories for your characters and speak in exotic accents. Retire to the bedroom and make your own romantic ending.

Nice

Love Poems

"How do I love thee? Let me count the ways..." Put your love for your mate into words with a little help from the experts.

❤ Seated in comfortable chairs in a quiet setting, spend time reading to each other from a book of love poetry, possibly John Donne's work or Elizabeth Barrett Browning's *Sonnets From the Portuguese*, a collection of love poems she dedicated to her husband.

❤ Now try your hand at writing love poems to each other, using images of your partner and memories of your times together. Write it on special paper from an art store and frame it, or make it small enough to fit in a wallet.

❤ You can also theme your evening around a work of literature, by dressing up like your favorite character from a book or movie and serving a meal like one the characters enjoyed in the story. The dining scenes in the movie *Pretty Woman* or the 1968 version of *Tom Jones* are classic scenes of seduction.

Naughty

Pot Boilers

Even if you or your mate isn't a big fan of reading, you won't find it boring when it's a book of erotic literature.

❤ Pick up a contemporary volume, like something by Anaïs Nin, a classic like Gustave Flaubert's *Madame Bovary*, or the ancient classic *Kama Sutra* for some helpful hints. You'll be surprised at what you'll find.

❤ Also peruse nonfiction how-to sex manuals, like *The Joy of Sex* by Alex Comfort or one of the books from William H. Masters and Virginia Johnson such as *Masters and Johnson on Sex and Human Loving*.

❤ Instructional sex videos will get you in the mood and give you ideas for trying new things in the bedroom, in the closet, on the coffee table, or wherever your new knowledge takes you. You can treat your "instruction" seriously or playfully. When it comes to the bedroom, who says learning can't be fun!

Nice

Interstate Escape

Nothing beats the freedom of being on the open road with the wind blowing through your hair. Grab your mate and get out on the highway!

❤ Choose a bright sunny day to borrow or rent a classic convertible or a Jeep Wrangler. Dress in your best sunglasses and tool along the coast or through the open countryside. Don't bother consulting a map; go where the wind takes you.

❤ Stop at a hot dog stand or greasy spoon to grab a bite. Explore roadside attractions and souvenir stands. Stop to see the "World's Biggest Ball of Twine." Purchase a tacky snow globe or ceramic salt shaker to remind you of your adventure.

❤ Challenge each other to car games. See how many different state license plates you can find, or play "I Spy." As evening approaches, pull to the side of the road and make a wish on the evening star.

Naughty

Joy Riding

Americans have long had a love affair with the automobile. It may be time to take your love affair on the road!

💜 Set off with your mate without a destination in mind, or flip a coin to determine which direction to go. Stick to the back roads in case you or your partner want to get a little risqué without raising too many eyebrows.

💜 Stop for lunch at a truck stop and flirt with your mate across the table. Play suggestive songs on the jukebox. Before you leave, journey to the restroom and buy novelty "rubbers" from the machine on the wall.

💜 In the early afternoon, start looking for a cheap motel for the night. Choose one with a big neon sign and "Magic Fingers" vibrating beds. Grab a roll of quarters at the desk and get ready to make your own magic!

Nice

Sunshine of My Life

Throw off those heavy winter clothes and get ready for summer! The sun's golden rays will cover every inch of your body with a warm blanket of sensual delight.

- Spend a relaxing day together at a pool, beach, lake, river, or ocean, soaking up the sun. Some sunscreen and a fashionable hat will allow you to have fun and be safe. There's plenty to do: swimming, sailing, surfing, hunting for seashells, and fishing.
- Or visit a resort that offers parasailing, scuba diving, cave diving, or hang-gliding. You could also try tandem parachuting, where you jump with a trained guide, or take lessons and go solo.
- Where's the best place in town to watch a sunrise? A sunset? Maybe it's a scenic overlook or a lake. Make plans to go watch these natural solar wonders. Be sure to take along lawn chairs, a blanket, and your favorite early-morning or late-night snacks.

Naughty

Bronze Beauties

The less clothing you wear, the more fun your day in the sun will be. Splurge on new bathing suits and cover-ups for your special getaway day.

♥ For proper protection, you'll need to put sunscreen all over each other. Do it lingeringly, lovingly, and frequently throughout the day. Later, to get it all off, take a shower together.

♥ The "towel attendant" scenario is a fun way to pretend you're at the seaside even when you're not. Have your mate go into a closet or bathroom, knock on the door, and announce that the towels you requested are here. Say you didn't ask for any. Then, while you're naked under the covers, have your partner come in while you explain that you didn't call. Towel attendants are very eager to please hotel guests.

♥ Or, at the beginning of your vacation, try out short-term self-tanning lotion on each other. To be convincing, you can't have tan lines!

Nice

Now You're Cookin'

Helping Mom in the kitchen has always been a magical experience for children. It's fun to watch all the ingredients being folded into the mix, especially when you get to lick the bowl!

❤ Spend a day together in the kitchen experimenting with a new recipe. Perhaps it is one your mate has seen in a cooking magazine or an old family favorite you have never tried. Remember, the shortest way to the heart is through the stomach!

❤ Go to the market with your partner and assemble all the ingredients. Make sure everything you need for the recipe is nearby. Play music in the kitchen to add to the setting.

❤ If you and your mate usually burn toast, you may want to take advantage of a non-cooking alternative. Visit a chili cook-off and sample all the secret recipes. Dine at the chef's table at a local restaurant and discover what it takes to prepare a gourmet meal.

going gourmet

Naughty

Recipe for Love

There is an old saying, "Kissin' don't last, but cookin' do." After spending some time in the kitchen together, you and your mate may beg to differ.

♥ Take an afternoon to create a meal that consists completely of aphrodisiacs. Through the years it has been thought that foods such as oysters, olives, and chocolate can increase a person's sex drive. It's time to put this theory to the test.

♥ Spice up the preparation of the meal even more by wearing only aprons and oven mitts. Seeing your mate naked in the kitchen may be all the aphrodisiac you need. Light candles to create a romantic mood for sharing your dinner. Make love on the dining room table.

♥ Another option is to create a smorgasbord of food that you can eat off of your partner's body. Warm sauces, melted chocolate,

cool gelatin, and whipped cream are all good choices. Bon appétit!

Nice

Food of the Gods

Every culture from the Aztecs on down has discovered the mysterious power of chocolate. Originally developed as a beverage, this rich, sweet confection comes in many forms today and is said to be an aphrodisiac.

❤ Visit several chocolate shops and sample the goods. Stop by the grocery store and buy a few of the different brands there. Back at home, compare them and see which ones you like best. Do the more expensive ones taste better? Which are your favorites: solids, cream centers, nut centers, or caramels? Light or dark? Take note of what your partner likes for future special occasions.

❤ Make a chocolate dessert at home that expresses your feelings for your mate. Build a monument to your love by arranging your partner's favorite desserts into a sculpture. Use snack cakes, fondue, hot cocoa, hot fudge sundaes, milkshakes, or brownies. Or share a real kiss for every Hershey's Kiss you eat! (If you can't indulge in chocolate, try a passion fruit tart.)

Naughty

A Chocolate Kiss

The love-enhancing properties of chocolate are legendary. Why is it that its smooth, rich taste always seems to leave us wanting more?

❤ No need to leave the house when you can bring the ice cream parlor in. Buy the fixings for ice cream sundaes, take them in the bedroom with your mate, and let your imagination do the rest. A can of whipped cream, chocolate sauce in a squeeze bottle, candy sprinkles, and nuts make a fabulous treat with you and your mate as the foundation.

❤ Or have a fondue party in bed. Get a bowl of chocolate syrup, along with strawberries, cherries, marshmallows, and pieces of banana. Dip and share. Don't be afraid to experiment.

❤ Check your local novelty or mail-order outlets for novelty chocolates. These anatomically correct treats can provide the perfect warm-up to lovemaking.

Nice

Make Mine Music

Music can set a mood of romance and help create memories that you and your mate will share for a long time to come. There may be no better selection than jazz.

❤ Plan an evening to see some live jazz music. Many areas have clubs that feature live performances. Treat your mate to dinner, and then head over to the club for martinis and some smooth music.

❤ Take advantage of the jazz offerings of a summer concert series. Pack a picnic basket full of cheeses and fresh fruits. Bring along a bottle of your favorite wine and a couple of glasses. Spread out a blanket and relax to the music beneath the stars.

❤ Ever dreamed of making your own music? Take music lessons with your mate. Find a reputable music teacher in your area that teaches piano, saxophone, or trumpet. It won't be long until you're making beautiful music together!

Naughty

In the Mood

Ever heard a song that reminds you of an erotic time that you have shared with your mate? Maybe it's time to jazz up your love life!

❤ Browse through an old record store with your partner. Look for classic recordings of Louis Armstrong, Ella Fitzgerald, or Billie Holiday. The scratchy quality of the vinyl recordings only adds to the mood.

❤ Spend an evening with the lights dimmed listening to your new musical finds. Close your eyes and let the music wash through you. Touch each other as if you are both fine instruments, capable of making the most beautiful music you have ever heard.

❤ If you and your mate are planning a vacation, visit the French Quarter in New Orleans. The combination of a quaint bed-and-breakfast and red-hot jazz is sure to make your bodies and spirits sing.

Nice

The Barter System

Going once, going twice, sold! The frenzy of the fast-talking auctioneer and the ever-increasing bids make auctions an exciting place to be, whether you're bidding or buying.

💜 Drive out into the country and attend a furniture auction or estate sale. It's a great way to see antiques and maybe add to your collection. You can also attend a livestock auction at a fair.

💜 For a night on the town, attend a fundraising dinner that includes a silent auction, where bidders write their names and bids on a list.

💜 Flea markets are great places to bargain for household miscellany as well as big-ticket items. Once you've honed your skills, practice them during a getaway to the Caribbean, South America, or the Middle East, where bartering for goods is part of the economy.

💜 Then build a sense of community in your own backyard by organizing a neighborhood bartering day, where you trade items such as produce, crafts, or home improvement services with your neighbors.

Naughty

Money Can Buy You Love
You can't put a price on love, but can you estimate it just for fun?

❤ Charities hold auctions for dates with eligible bachelors or bachelorettes, usually local TV celebrities. Hold one at home! Have your partner dress up in formal attire and model it for you. Describe his or her qualifications the way a master of ceremonies would do. How much are you willing to bid?

❤ Or have a silent auction, using as auction items activities you especially enjoy during lovemaking. Take six sheets of paper,

three for each of you, and write at the top one thing you would like to do with your partner. List the value of each at $25.

❤ Now, put the lists out on a table. With each of you having $75 to spend, go around the table and write down your bids in $5 increments. How much of your funds you are willing to invest in getting this "item"? When you're both out of bidding money, see which activities come up as the winners, and pay up!

Nice

Creative Cantina
There are many ways to experience the culture of our southern neighbors. Take some time to mix things up with a Mexican flair!

- Create a Mexican feast for family and friends. Prepare tacos, burritos, and tamales. Experiment with fresh salsa recipes to please everyone, from those who like mild flavor to those who like it fiery.
- Enjoy a night out at an authentic Mexican restaurant with your mate. Share a margarita or a glass of homemade sangria. Tip the musicians and they may serenade your partner right at the table.
- Plan a trip to Mexico. There are several ways to see this beautiful country. All-inclusive resorts offer all your activities and meals at one reasonable price. Cruises of the western Caribbean often include a stop in a Mexican location. If you are visiting the southwest United States, drive across the border and explore an open-air market for the day.

Naughty

Spice It Up

Has your love life been getting a bit chilly lately? Tap into your potential heat with a touch of Mexico!

💜 Create your own personal Mexican festival at home. Surprise your mate with midnight margaritas. Make frozen margaritas and share them right from the blender. Play Latin-flavored music and hold your partner close as you tango around the kitchen.

💜 Perform a Mexican hat dance for your mate. Spice up your routine by slowly removing articles of clothing until there's nothing left but a sombrero.

💜 Settle into a Mexican blanket that has been spread out on the floor. Share body shots with your partner. First, lick and salt your mate's neck and place a lime in your mate's mouth. Drink a shot of tequila, quickly lick and share the lime. The combination of the tequila, salt, lime, and your mate's lips should heat things up "south of the border"!

Nice

Rain on the Roof

A gentle rain makes us contemplative; a thunderstorm makes us want to snuggle under the covers within our partner's safe embrace.

❤ The next time it rains, crawl into bed together and spend the day reading, snuggling, and listening to your favorite relaxing music. Whip up your favorite snacks and bring them to bed as well. This is one time that eating crackers in bed is allowed. As the rain subsides, go outside and listen to it gently falling on the leaves. Is there a rainbow?

❤ Turn out all the lights and illuminate the bedroom only with candles. Open the curtains or blinds and watch the storm outside. Use this quiet time for reflection, sharing memories of the first time you met. Tell each other how you felt then and how those feelings have strengthened with time.

❤ If you're really brave, watch a movie about a storm, like *Twister, The Wizard of Oz*, or *Hurricane*.

#

Thunder in Paradise

The intensity of pounding rain and the thunder it brings makes many lovers amorous.

- ❤ Brave the rain and go for a walk together. Splash in the puddles, then stop under a tree and kiss. Now find a private place and make love with the rain pouring down upon you. Continue your wet passion with a shower together.
- ❤ Or use your vehicle as your love nest. Drive to a remote area and make love while the rain beats down. Or express your passion while the car's in the garage.
- ❤ If you're at the beach, make love as the surf crashes over you, à la that famous scene in *From Here to Eternity*. Or enjoy passionate lovemaking on the beach at night in the crackling heat of a bonfire.
- ❤ For a bigger adventure, take a trip to a tropical setting and make love in a cascading waterfall or in the pool of your own private corner of an island oasis.

Nice

Tidy Up

The mere mention of housework can strike fear into the heart of even the most organized person. Why not take some of the headache out of your weekly chores and have a little fun at the same time?

- ❤ Sit down and make a list of housework that you and your mate can do as a team. Over the weekend, get up early and begin to tackle the list together. Give yourselves a small reward, like a tall glass of lemonade, each time a task is completed.

- ❤ Add more challenge to your list of chores by setting a time limit for each item on your list. As a team, try to beat the clock. Not only will you have a great time, your cleaning will be accomplished much faster.

- ❤ Work at a small project together. Visit a local home improvement store for needed materials. When the project is completed, revel together in the feeling of a job well done.

Naughty

Squeaky Clean

Ever imagine cleaning your house as an erotic adventure? Didn't think so, but with a little ingenuity, housework can become much more fun.

❤ Next time you do laundry, make sure to put all your clothes into the wash. Strip for each other in the laundry room as you prepare the washing machine. Making love on top during the spin cycle might make laundry the highlight of your week.

❤ Vacuuming and dusting can be much more interesting when done in the nude. Some companies offer a similar service, but doing it yourself adds that extra personal touch. For an added thrill, lightly run your feather duster over your mate's bare skin.

❤ Clean the bathroom together. Work your way into the shower with your partner. Make sure to give everything a good cleaning, including each other. Hey, don't forget the grout!

Nice

Chance Encounter

Remember the excitement of the romantic love that you felt when you first met your mate? Relive that feeling with a set-up chance encounter.

💜 Tell your mate to meet you in a hotel bar, but not to sit with you upon arriving. Catch your mate's eye when he or she arrives, but then look away, as though you're interested but coy. How long will it be before your partner just has to come over for introductions? Talk as though you are total strangers. What would you ask someone you've just met? Let the conversation continue through dinner.

💜 At the end of the evening, which one of you will say first that you would like to see each other again? Kiss passionately when you part and exchange phone numbers on napkins.

💜 Did you learn anything new about each other by talking as though you were strangers? It can seem that we know almost everything about a person until we take on a new perspective.

Naughty

Come Here Often?

Play out your sexual fantasies about one-night stands within the privacy of your own relationship.

- ❤ Send your mate an "anonymous" invitation via phone, fax, pager, email, or letter, to meet you in a hotel bar. In the message, say you've been admiring your partner and what you find so sexy.

- ❤ Meet in the bar wearing an exciting outfit and the sexiest underwear you can find (or none!). Have a sexually suggestive conversation, as though you are two strangers interested in having a good time for the night.

- ❤ To prolong the anticipation, have appetizers or dinner together, maybe in the hotel restaurant. Keep building the suggestive nature of your conversation. Have it lead to your getting a room and making love as though it's your first time together.

Nice

Higher Learning

Do you have fond memories of attending pep rallies, borrowing your parents' car, or going to the senior prom? Throw on your school jacket and take your mate on a trip down memory lane.

❤ Pull out your old school yearbooks and browse through them with your partner. Share humorous stories as you look over pictures of old classmates.

❤ Put together a field trip to visit your mate's high school or college campus. Stroll through the old buildings, have lunch in a favorite hangout, or buy a souvenir from the bookstore.

❤ If it's impossible to visit your alma mater, attend a local homecoming game or other sporting event. Cheer the home team on to victory, then take your mate out for sodas and a pizza.

❤ If you are yearning to get back in the classroom, find a subject that interests you and take a class together. Think of the study dates!

school days

Sex Education

Were you or your mate a late bloomer? Ever considered a wall-flower at school dances? Well, let's make up for lost time!

- 💜 Go back to see old friends at your class reunion. Make sure you and your partner are dressed to the nines. Set out to dazzle everyone in attendance. Spend the evening sharing stories with old school chums. Raise a few eyebrows by dancing provocatively to slow songs. Make out with your mate in the corner.

- 💜 Or stage a school dance in your home. Decorate with streamers and balloons. Play old favorites to dance to. At the end of the evening, don't keep your date wondering about a good night kiss.

- 💜 Drive out to your local "lover's lane." Go parking like you did in high school. Make out in the back seat like a couple of teenagers. The best part is you won't have to worry about missing your curfew!

Nice

A Taste of the Islands
Clear blue water, white sand beaches, and spectacular black volcanoes create the lure of Hawaii.

❤ Have your own Hawaiian luau without even leaving the house! Get decked out in Hawaiian shirts and shorts, sandals, and straw hats. Pick up some plastic or silk-flower leis at a party store.

❤ For your feast, prepare baked ham or roast pork covered in a glaze of pineapple, mango, and papaya. Whip up blender drinks of coconut milk and top them off with little paper umbrellas.

❤ Crank up the Hawaiian music or play Elvis's movie *Blue Hawaii* in the background.

❤ For some fun that takes a little muscle, buy a real coconut and extract the milk. Punch a hole in each of the three "eyes," or dark round spots. To get at the coconut, heat the whole thing for fifteen minutes in an oven at 350 degrees. Then tap it all over with a hammer, remove the shell and the brown skin, and toast the coconut in pieces for seven to ten minutes.

Tropical Paradise

They say the hula dancer's hands tell the story, although the hips appear to play a pivotal role as well. For a romantic evening, turn your bedroom into a tropical nighttime paradise.

- ♥ At a party store, buy grass skirts and plastic or silk leis to wear as necklaces or wrapped twice around your head for a floral wreath. Import stores have seashell jewelry that will make a seductive rhythm on your ankles and wrists.
- ♥ Buy several yards of tropical print fabric and have fun seeing how many outfits you can make for each other by wrapping it around your naked bodies. Or just wear swimsuits.
- ♥ Now, mix up your favorite tropical drinks and serve them in fake coconut drinking cups. Position large candles around the room to imitate tiki torches. Spray hibiscus or gardenia cologne in the air. Unroll a straw or reed mat on the floor, start the Hawaiian music, and rub coconut-scented lotion on each other.

Nice

Casino Royale

Casinos have a seductive atmosphere uniquely their own. The whir of roulette wheels, the bright, flashing neon lights, and the feel of crisp playing cards all lend to the mystique. Try any of these ideas to ensure that you're a big winner!

- ❤ Plan an evening out with your mate at a nearby casino. Coastal areas offer short gambling cruises, and many reservations have casinos. If it's not possible to travel to one of these locations, local groups often host themed "Casino Nights."
- ❤ As an alternative, plan a night of cards in your home. Invite friends and family for an evening of bridge or poker. Borrow several card tables and serve drinks and light snacks like chips and pretzels.
- ❤ Arrange to take part in a group trip to Las Vegas or Atlantic City. Look for inexpensive packages that include travel and accommodations. These destinations also have many non-gambling activities available.

Naughty

Lucky in Love
Roll the dice, spin the wheel, and take a chance on love!

❤ Create an evening of casino fun, where Lady Luck always comes out on top. Plan several games of chance that can be played by two. Raise the stakes on blackjack by wagering intimate favors as the payoff. A feverish game of strip poker is sure to lead to jackpot winnings.

❤ Visit an adult novelty shop with your mate and pick out a game designed for lovers. A set of romantic dice or love lottery tickets will bring out the gambler in both of you.

❤ Log on to an online casino and play the interactive slot machines. Don't play for money; kisses or sexual advances will make the game much more fun.

❤ Purchase a roll of lottery tickets and curl up in bed with your partner. Negotiate a romantic interlude with your winnings. Who said money can't buy love?

Nice

The Long, Hot Summer
The hot climate of the South makes for a laid-back lifestyle. Adopt that sultry attitude for an evening or a day with your mate.

❤ On the next warm day, put on your crispest white cotton clothing and lie on lounge chairs outside, fanning each other with a magazine or newspaper. Sip mint juleps, iced tea, or fresh lemonade.

❤ To satisfy your hunger for something Southern, dig into some warm peach or pecan pie with ice cream melted on top. Or have the classic Southern snack combination of a Moon Pie snack cake and an RC Cola.

❤ Then head indoors to watch *The Long, Hot Summer*, *Cat on a Hot Tin Roof*, or another sassy Southern favorite. Read parts of a Tennessee Williams play to each other.

❤ Later on, take a road trip, Southern style, by throwing a picnic lunch in a rented pick-up truck and driving on country roads until you find the perfect shady spot under a spreading oak tree. Or have the picnic in the truck bed.

Southern Nights

Evenings in the South are warm, and the stickiness of the air is best handled by donning your skimpiest warm-weather attire and enjoying some cold drinks together.

❤ Turn the lights off, light the candles, and drape your bed with gauze or cheesecloth, creating your own Southern-style love nest, where the gauze keeps out mosquitoes. Grab a basin of water, crush eucalyptus or camphor leaves in it, and give each other cooling sponge baths in bed.

❤ Add the flavor of Southern casinos to your night by playing poker or another card game. Play ragtime or jazz music in the background.

❤ For a taste of rustic living, rent a cabin at a fishing camp for the weekend. Cruise the river or lake in a rowboat, then stroll along the shore in the moonlight. Find a secluded spot and get back to nature by going for a skinny dip. Fish bite before dawn, so get up before the birds for some early morning love-making, then head outside to catch your own breakfast.

Nice

Sky's the Limit
Air travel has long been a fascination for those who are adventurous at heart. Charles Lindbergh and Amelia Earhart have flown into history as figures of romance and mystery.

❤ Make plans for an exhilarating trip into the clouds. Schedule an early morning hot air balloon ride for you and your mate. Marvel at the countryside as you float peacefully through the air. Ask about including a delicious brunch as part of your experience.

❤ Charter a plane or helicopter ride. Tour your surrounding area from the air. If you'd rather keep your feet firmly planted on the ground, tour a small local airport or aviation museum. Air shows are another great way to share your love of flight.

❤ For a daring change of pace, take flying lessons or go skydiving to tap into your mate's inner daredevil. Have your adventure videotaped to share with family and friends.

up, up, and away

Naughty

Wild Blue Yonder

Are you and your mate thrilled by thoughts of soaring far above the ground? Indulge in an aviation fantasy and keep your love flying high!

❤ Meet your mate's returning flight with a sensual surprise. If your local airport includes a hotel, check into a room and make love to the sound of aircraft taking off. (Splurge and book the penthouse suite.)

❤ Many areas have a road near the airport where curious locals park to watch the airplanes depart and land. Go parking at dusk and make out like teenagers beneath the roar of the jet engines.

❤ Visit a surplus store and purchase a parachute to spread out on your bed. Make love enshrouded in its billowing softness.

❤ Watch a space shuttle launch from the comfort of your bed. Time your lovemaking so you and your mate "take off" with the shuttle. No problem here, Houston!

Nice

A Perfect Match
Are there cosmic forces at work that have brought the two of you together? If so, what else can they tell you?

❤ Read your horoscopes or numerology report from a newspaper, magazine, or Internet site. Do further research on what each of your signs means, how they complement each other, and where there might be trouble spots.

❤ Go a step further into the unknown by having a psychic, palmist, I-Ching practitioner, astrologer, or numerologist tell your fortunes, or call one of the television psychics. Do your own tarot card reading by buying a set of cards and a book of their meanings. You can also buy a set of Chinese fortune sticks.

❤ To really go beyond, attend a past life regression, a session in which some people believe you find out who you were in a previous life. Now tie all of this information together. How can it make you more compatible?

Naughty

You Will Meet a Tall, Dark Stranger

There are those who have mysterious powers to tell fortunes and predict the destinies of lovers. Put your own psychic powers to work on each other.

- ❤ The fortune-teller should wear the best in thrift-store garb: white cotton shirt or blouse, long black skirt or slacks, head scarf, big gold hoop earrings, and jangling bracelets. The customer should wear a sexy outfit.

- ❤ Set up a round table in the center of a room and cover it with a cloth. Light only one candle in the darkened room to make the ambience mysterious. Make your own crystal ball by filling a translucent glass light fixture globe with crumpled tissue paper and turning it upside down in the center of the table.

- ❤ As you read the fortune by way of tarot cards, crystal ball, or fortune-telling sticks, make the talk sexually suggestive. Have the gypsy foretell that you are destined for a romantic encounter that very evening.

Nice

It's in the Stars
What mysteries do the stars hold for you and your mate? Take time to investigate their shimmering possibilities together.

❤ Visit a local planetarium with your partner. Many science centers schedule daily programs that point out the amazing features of the night sky.

❤ Join a stargazing group on an outing to view the twinkling jewels that exist light-years from earth. Purchase a telescope and share the wonders from your own backyard.

❤ Plan a meeting with an astrologer and learn what the stars have in store for you and your mate. Go to a bookstore and research your zodiac signs. Do they really reflect your passions and desires?

❤ The best idea would be to spend the evening close to the one you love discovering the stars in your partner's eyes!

heavenly bodies

In Orbit

Arrange some time to send your love life into the stratosphere!

💜 Pick a clear evening to get away from the lights of your city or town. Drive out into the country for an evening of stargazing. Pack a snack, a bottle of wine, and a soft, comfortable blanket. Make love illuminated only by starlight.

💜 Create your own sexy solar system at home. Purchase glow-in-the-dark stars and place them all over the ceiling of your bedroom. Another idea is to make your own star machine with a large tin can and small lamp. Carefully punch tiny holes in the can and place it over the lamp. Spend the evening exploring new worlds with your partner.

💜 Investigate having a star named after your mate. During a special dinner, present your partner with a certificate naming the star. You'll likely be rewarded with a trip into the heavens!

Nice

Can't Scare Me

Telling ghost stories around a campfire is a camping tradition. Whose heart doesn't race at hearing the story of the Headless Horseman from "The Legend of Sleepy Hollow" or the terrifying events from a scary movie?

❤ Probe the recesses of your brain for ghost stories you know from childhood and research new ones. Have your partner do the same, but don't tell each other yet! Now, camp out in your living room, using only the fireplace or a cluster of candles as your campfire. As you tell your stories, hold a flashlight under your chin on the especially scary parts.

❤ Then take a nighttime excursion to a haunted place in your town. Is it an abandoned house? The scene of a crime? A cemetery? Gather your best ghost-hunting gear, including wooden stakes and a camera, and see how much investigating you can do before you head for the safety of your ghost-busting vehicle!

Naughty

Ghoulish Garb

While we mortals sleep, the nighttime world of ghosts and goblins comes to life. Are you ready to enter their domain?

❤ See if you can spend the night in a tent alone together in your backyard, at a campground, or even in your living room. There's nothing sexier than being naked together in one sleeping bag.

❤ Explore another part of your personality by going shopping for clothing that suits the wilder side of you, such as Goth or vampire apparel or bondage duds. It's available at party stores, specialty  boutiques, novelty stores, and through mail order. Buy outfits without revealing what you've purchased. Then take turns surprising each other wearing them, maybe one of you debuting your outfit one weekend and the other the next.

❤ To be really daring, wear your new clothing to a bar or nightclub that is the hangout of people who follow this lifestyle.

Nice

Dreamweaver
How often do you and your mate share your dreams with each other? Take some time out to make those dreams become reality.

❤ Spend the day together discovering each other's fondest wishes. Dreams come in many forms and can be as simple or extravagant as you choose. Make plans to make some of these dreams come true. Come up with creative ways of fulfilling your shared fantasies.

❤ Visit someone who specializes in dream analysis and learn about your mate's innermost passions and desires. Purchase a book and spend the afternoon analyzing your dreams.

❤ Pick a day to eliminate all external distractions. Don't schedule any appointments and unplug the telephone. Snuggle in your mate's arms and slip off to dreamland.

Naughty

Cloud Nine

What does your dream world look like? Perhaps you dream of lovers being suspended in a marshmallow cloud, where they share a sensual embrace. Create a heavenly setting in your home for an evening of dream-like romance.

❤ Transform your bedroom into a white, fluffy cloud. Drape the walls with loose hanging white sheets. A soft feather bed and cool cotton sheets only add to the atmosphere. Fill the bed with various-sized pillows.

❤ Light the room with candles and play soft New Age music. Dress yourself in a silky white negligee or satin robe. Add a hint of fragrance to complete the room.

❤ When your mate arrives, place a finger to your partner's lips to indicate that no words need be spoken. It won't be long before you both realize that dreams can come true!

Nice

Relive That Special Day

Anniversaries are usually celebrated by exchanging gifts and going out to dinner. Why not make the day more special by affirming your love for each other in a grander way?

❤ Plan a ceremony for just the two of you, or with friends and family, to renew your love. Find the vows you originally read, or go to the bookstore or library for new vows that express how you feel now. Hold the ceremony at a place that has special meaning for you, perhaps the place where you were married, the place where you met, or a spot of scenic beauty. Use the same colors, cake, music, and invitations you used before. This is a chance to relive the first ceremony or to make it your dream or fantasy ceremony.

❤ For a second honeymoon, go to a traditionally romantic place like Niagara Falls, the Caribbean, Hawaii, or Mexico. Or go bigger: to Europe, Australia, Thailand, or Bali.

Countdown to Love

Let's face it—the wedding is fun, but the honeymoon is the pay-off!

💜 Do a strip-club version of your wedding for just the two of you. Put on only the hats, jewelry, and shoes that you wore for your wedding and meet each other in the bedroom. Reread your vows, then have a champagne toast with arms entwined and a cake feeding ceremony. Get as wild as you want.

💜 Resorts in the Poconos Mountains and Las Vegas are famous for their honeymoon suites that feature heart-shaped or round beds and even bathtubs that are giant champagne glasses. For low-budget fun, get a room at a cheap hotel that's notorious for its hourly rates and mirrored ceilings.

💜 Or create your own naughty activities based on the list of anniversary gifts promoted by card stores: leather is the traditional gift for the third anniversary and the modern gift for the ninth; lace is the modern gift for the eighth; appliances are the modern gift for the fourth.

Nice

Picture It

Has anyone ever told you that you ought to be in pictures? Well, now is a perfect time to start.

- ♥ Many couples use photographs to mark important celebrations such as engagements and weddings. Start using photos to celebrate every day of your relationship.

- ♥ Arrange to have photographs of you and your mate taken at a studio or department store. Make the photos special by choosing a favorite outfit for each other to wear.

- ♥ Buy disposable cameras and go to a nearby park or city for a fun-filled photo session. Snap candid shots beneath a shady tree or near a bubbling fountain. Ask someone to take a few pictures of the two of you.

- ♥ Black and white film can add an air of romance to your photos. Purchase a special album to fill with your new memories.

Naughty

Sexy Snapshots
Does the thought of a scantily clad picture of your mate send your blood pulsing? A sexy photo session may be just what is needed.

💙 Several companies offer "boudoir" photography services, but taking the pictures at home is sure to be more fun. Put together a backdrop where your model will be posing. Create a pleasing atmosphere with some romantic music for your mate to work with.

💙 Choose several racy outfits to be modeled. Give your partner pointers while in front of the camera. Urge your mate to get comfortable and remove some articles of clothing. When your have captured the images you want, switch places. After all, turnabout is fair play!

💙 If your camera is equipped with a timer, you may want to take some pictures of the two of you together. As they say in the "biz," make love to the camera!

Nice

Back to the Olden Days
Can you imagine life without electricity? What about just for a day?

❤ Have fun with this idea by pretending you don't have electricity for an afternoon or an evening. What can you do for fun? For starters, cover all your clocks, then get out your battery-operated radio or open the windows and listen to the sounds of your neighborhood.

❤ To communicate the old-fashioned way, rig up two empty soup cans and a string and try talking to each other by shutting the string in the door between two rooms.

❤ If it's cold, snuggle together under the blankets to conserve heat. If it's hot, use hand-held fans and mist each other with cool water.

❤ Play games together that don't require electricity, such as board games, card games, or charades. Toward evening, light some candles and have a shadow puppet show, construct a fort or tent using a blanket stretched over a table, and roast marshmallows in the fireplace.

Naughty

Feel Your Way
Making love in the dark adds a sense of mystery to the encounter.

❤ Turn out all the lights, pull the curtains, and make the room as dark as possible. Then meet each other in bed and put on blindfolds. Using only your senses of touch, smell, and taste, find each other and make mad, passionate love without ever making eye contact.

❤ Or, get in bed wearing a blindfold and have your mate appear in the room as a mysterious stranger you would want to meet. Playing the game "Twenty Questions," figure out who this mysterious stranger is. It could be a celebrity, historical figure, or character from a movie. Once you find out, welcome that person into your bed and make love. Have your mate leave a rose on the pillow upon departing.

❤ For a quick activity, play hide and seek in your house, in the nude.

Nice

Sounds of Silence

A knowing glance; a welcome smile; a long embrace. Any one of these things can be worth a thousand words. Why not spend some time with your mate without uttering a word?

💛 Choose a quiet activity for an afternoon of leisure. Curl up in a big easy chair together with some good books. Share stolen glances over the pages of your favorite literary work.

💛 Purchase stationary and discover the lost art of letter writing together. Compose notes to old friends, stopping to wink playfully at your mate.

💛 Make plans for a whole day of silence. Disconnect the phone and don't answer the door. Share an afternoon of silent movies. If you must venture into public, communicate with notes or your own body language.

💛 Attend a sign-language class together and learn how to communicate without a word. If nothing else, take time to quietly look into each other's eyes. What you find there will mean more than any words.

Language of Love

Have you ever finished your mate's sentences? Do you sometimes have the same thought at the exact same time? You may have developed your own lover's language.

- ❤ Become fluent in the international language of love. Plan an intimate encounter that takes place in complete silence. Let your mate know what you long for with a simple gesture or action.

- ❤ Place your lover's hands on your body and show your partner what gets you excited. In exchange, linger over your mate's sensual areas. Making love in the absence of sound may heighten your other senses.

- ❤ Challenge your mate to a romantic game of "Mum." See which of you can remain speechless the longest. Set the stakes high. Perhaps the winner's sexual fantasy will be fulfilled. Do everything in your power to break your partner's silence. A long, slow striptease or hot-oil massage may ensure your victory. Remember that all is fair in love and war!

Nice

Small Favors

A spontaneous, unexpected gift of love reminds us of how much our partner cares.

♥ Buy or make three small gifts that represent aspects of your relationship, and have your partner do the same. Choose three objects: one that will feed your partner's mind, one that will nourish the body, and one that will bolster the soul. The gifts may be things like a magazine or book your partner has been wanting to read, a favorite candy, or a gold charm of something significant to you both.

♥ Wrap each one individually and label them Something For Your Mind, Something For Your Body, and Something For Your Soul.

♥ Present the gifts to each other over dinner, taking turns opening the corresponding ones. Share smiles and heartfelt hugs. Talk about why you chose the items you did.

Naughty

Naughty Novelties
What three things could you buy that would liven up your love life? Buy or make three items that will add a spark.

❤ Visit a novelty store or shop online to find three naughty items to share with each other. Do this separately so you won't know what your partner is planning. You might be surprised at what's available: lingerie, lotions, oils, toys for men and women, suggestively-shaped candies, sex-enhancing foods, bondage accessories, edible underwear, vibrators, videos, and magazines. When you receive the items, wrap them and label them Naughty, Very Naughty, and Naughtiest.

❤ On some special evening, take a shower or bath together, then get into bed and open the gifts. Which ones will you start with? Try out each one after you open it, even if it takes you all night.

Nice

Raise a Glass

If you enjoy sharing a tall, frosty mug of beer or a bottle of fine wine with your mate, make plans to learn more about your favorite beverages.

❤ Visit a local brewery or vineyard and discover all the effort that goes into the creation of these delicious indulgences. Explore the romance that has surrounded the making of beer and wine through the ages.

❤ Attend a beer festival or celebration of Bacchus. Sample delectable foods and lose yourselves in the dancing and revelry or host a beer or wine tasting in your home. Ask your guests to bring a favorite for sharing.

❤ Purchase a beer-making kit and create your own special homemade brew. Give your creation a name that says something about you and your mate.

❤ Take a wine-tasting class together. Learn to pair wine perfectly with different dishes. Eat, drink, and be merry!

Naughty

Liquor Is Quicker

The Greeks thought of wine as a gift from the gods. Don't overlook this gift when planning your next romance rendezvous with your mate.

❤ Share a bottle of wine by candlelight beneath the stars. Set up a small bistro table in your backyard. Complete the setting with glowing candles. Hold each other close and ponder the night sky while sipping fragrant wine.

❤ Indulge in a sinfully decadent champagne bubble bath. The mixture of bubbles and bubbly are a surefire equation for a sensual evening.

❤ Recapture your wild college days with a beer-drinking game. Challenge your mate to a lively game of "Quarters." The object of the game is to bounce a quarter into a shot glass full of beer. When players are successful, their opponent must drink the beer. Any inhibitions will soon melt away.

❤ Treat your partner to a luxurious bath including a beer hair wash. Cheers!

Nice

Hooked on You

When you're in love, you feel connected to your mate in body, mind, and spirit. Now try it literally, by spending all or part of the day linked together.

❤ Hook a bungee cord or a long spiral keychain to your belt loops. Now have some crazy fun as you eat breakfast side-by-side, complete some chores, watch TV, and other activities you'd normally do.

❤ Talk about the things that make you feel especially connected to each other, like childhood experiences you may both have had or events you've shared since you've been together.

❤ If you're brave, go out into the world! Take a walk or a run, or visit a school playground and go down the slide while hooked together. You might even want to visit a carnival or fair, where the environment is a little more relaxed to begin with. Take advantage of two-for-one specials at bars and restaurants!

Naughty

Captain Hook

Being together always takes on a new meaning when you hook yourselves together for some naughty fun!

💗 Purchase toy handcuffs, which come in plastic or metal, for fun in the bedroom. Novelty stores sell them fur-lined for that balance of pleasure and "pain." Other kinds of stores have even more chain-related items that you might want to experiment with. Or use a bungee cord or plastic spiral keychain.

💗 Get in bed together naked and hook yourselves up with all of the chains, handcuffs, ribbons, and scarves that you have. Make love as captives of your bondage.

💗 Or take turns, with one of you held prisoner and the other in charge of "torturing" with a feather. Prisoners always try to please their guards in order to negotiate an escape.

Nice

The Eyes Have It
People often take what they see for granted. Why not spend a day seeing the world through the eyes of your mate?

- Instruct your mate to wear a blindfold for your day together. If your partner is concerned about the stares a blindfold may elicit, use dark sunglasses and tightly closed eyes instead.
- Take time to describe the people you encounter and your surroundings. Halfway through the day, switch places. By evening, you're sure to have a new appreciation of each other.
- With your mate blindfolded, watch a movie together at home. Describe the action, the colors, and whatever other visual elements your partner may be missing.
- Later, remove the blindfold and spend the evening lost in each other's eyes. Keep in mind, these activities are for your eyes only!

love is blind

Naughty

Sensual Senses

When you met your mate, was it love at first sight? Arrange an encounter that will put the theory that out of sight is out of mind to rest forever.

❤ Meet your lover at the door with a blindfold. Gently cover your mate's eyes while whispering reassurances. Lead your partner into the bedroom by the hand.

❤ Describe what is happening as you undress. Add to the anticipation by tossing an undergarment to your mate. Increase your partner's sense of touch by using different textures, such as silk sheets or a feather boa, during lovemaking.

❤ Stage a blind taste test. Assemble a variety of sensual foods. Fresh melon wedges, strawberries, chocolate, and vanilla ice cream are perfect. Feed each other and savor the different tastes. Combine flavors by kissing passionately.

❤ When the blindfold is removed, your mate will fall in love all over again.

Nice

Your Better Half

Want to find out how the other half—your better half—lives? Try stepping into each other's shoes for a day and see what life is like from the other side.

❤ Sit down together and make a list of your regular responsibilities for the day. Now switch them! You do everything on your mate's "to do" list and vice versa. Maybe you can meet up for lunch and get any advice you need. At lunch, have each other's favorite food.

❤ When you're all done, relax on the couch wearing each other's pajamas and watch *Freaky Friday, Trading Places*, or *Big*.

❤ For a grander switcheroo, look into exchanging your home with another couple for the weekend or a week. What part of the country would you love to vacation in? You can find home-exchange services on the Internet that screen clients and match them with similar couples. Be sure to get recommendations from current customers.

trading places

Naughty

Role Reversal

Get out of your routine in the bedroom by trading places there as well. If you normally initiate lovemaking, have your partner do it. If you have your standard positions and activities, come up with some fresh, creative ones.

❤ Instead of just stepping into each other's shoes, slip into something even more comfortable—each other's clothes! Yes, from head to toe, try on your partner's clothes, underwear and all. If the sizes aren't right, go buy some that are. Some couples take this farther, into a role play, and find it to be a lot of fun.

❤ For a walk on the wilder side, rent a video or see a show featuring female impersonators and other cross-dressers, or visit a store or website that features clothes for people who

dress across gender. Did you discover anything about the advantages and disadvantages of the other sex?

Nice

Never Say Never

Are there things that you have always wanted to do with your mate, but never find time for? Well, not for long!

💜 Create a bulletin board of activities that you have never shared with your mate. Let your imagination run wild. No idea is too small or too large. Write each idea on an index card and attach it to the board.

💜 Using a dart or other means, randomly select a card. Drop everything and do that activity immediately. Don't move on to your next idea until you have completed the one that was chosen.

💜 Make a list together of the things you will never do to each other. Use phrases like, "I will never laugh at you when you are down," or, " I will never leave you alone." Post the list or keep a copy with you so that you will see it every day. You will never be lacking for creative ways to spend time together again.

i never

Naughty

Never Neverland

What are your heart's deepest desires? What unspoken ecstasies do you wish for? There has never been a better time than the present to share these with your mate.

❤ Choose an evening to lie in bed and share "I Never" phrases. Begin each thought with the words "I never…" Talk candidly about the sexual feelings and urges that your lover has awakened within you.

❤ End your conversation by whispering into your mate's ear, "I never thought I could love someone as much as I love you." That's one less thing you have never done!

❤ Plan an evening to play simple competitive games, such as tic-tac-toe or checkers. Inform your mate that the winner gets to share a sexual fantasy that they have never experienced. It is the loser's duty to make sure that this fantasy becomes reality. With a reward like this, you'll forget who the loser is!

Nice

Give Me a Clue

Everyone loves the thrill of the hunt, even if it's just when you're shopping! Create your own search mission at home by having a love-themed scavenger hunt for the two of you.

❤ Buy a small gift or treat to hide somewhere in your home. The prize can be a coupon for a kiss or an offer to do a chore for your partner. Now, develop a series of ten clues to get your mate from the starting point through a trail of clever stops along the way, ultimately leading to the prize. Write the clues in clever ways to make it difficult. Maybe you can write them as short poems. Or you can include a compliment about your partner on each.

❤ Tricky places to hide clues include in a shoe, under a placemat, and in the pockets of your mate's pants. When the clues are hidden, bring your partner in, introduce the game with the first clue—and send your mate hunting! You can set a time limit if you like the competitive spirit.

Me, Tarzan

Who knows what animal instincts lie just beneath the surface of your mate's calm exterior? Have your partner embark on a lusty quest with you as the prize.

- Don your best safari-themed lingerie for this hunt. Animal-print underwear and scarves, along with boots and a whip, make for an exciting adventure.
- Now, hide a series of items—such as sexy undergarments or naughty pictures—throughout your home. Write a series of spicy clues on pieces of paper that will lead your mate from place to place. With each clue, include a brief sexy activity that you have to do before going to the next clue. What will the grand prize be?
- Write a different letter of the alphabet on the back of each clue which, when put together, spell the special thing you and your mate will do in bed when the scavenger hunt is over. Happy hunting!

Nice

Right on Time

With today's busy schedules, it is hard to find time to spend with the one you love. Business meetings and household chores gobble up our waking hours. Believe it or not, time is on your side!

- ❤ Make time stand still. Put away your watch and cover the clocks. Spend the whole day together without once knowing what time it is. Make no plans and just enjoy your mate's company.

- ❤ If you like the thrill of beating time at its own game, select several activities to accomplish during the day. Set a time limit for each activity. When time expires on one activity, move on to the next. You'll be amazed at what can be accomplished.

- ❤ If you live in an area where the time changes in the fall, use the time you gain to do something frivolous with your mate. Slow dance beneath the harvest moon or make spiced apple cider. It's okay. You have time.

Timeless Romance

Have you ever heard it said that time is a thief? Take matters into your own hands and steal back some of this precious commodity!

- ❤ With your newfound time, have a lovemaking marathon. Engage in some extended foreplay and see how long you can make your passionate encounter last. Or if time is still an issue, squeeze a "quickie" into your busy schedule.
- ❤ Plan some "topsy-turvy time." Spend the entire day in bed. Of course, sleeping is optional. Rise at sunset and be night owls together. Take care of your regular daily activities, like shopping at a twenty-four-hour supermarket.
- ❤ Gather twenty-four slips of paper and write an hour of the day on each one. Place all the slips into a hat and draw out two or three slips. During the day, stop whatever you are doing and make love at the selected times. Now every hour can be happy hour!

Nice

You've Got Mail

Computers offer exciting avenues for information and communication. Use them to add some fun to your relationship.

❤ Subscribe to an online service that gives you your own free web page. Then design it together and put your favorite photos on it, or post information about your interests. Tell friends and family to check out what's going on in your lives!

❤ Need a new computer, piece of equipment, or software? Go shopping together, then come home and install your purchase. Visit a computer show to see what's new. Take advantage of demonstrations of hardware and software.

❤ For a fun evening, surf the net for websites that are of interest to you both, or search for the word "romance" and see what ideas you get.

Online and in Love

Electronic communication provides a cloak of mystery for your romantic interludes.

💜 Using separate email addresses, send messages to each other with the purpose of leading to a seduction. Come up with sexy nicknames to use online. Start the exchange with get-to-know-you messages, but then make them more and more racy. Describe yourself in exaggerated terms. Talk about what you'll do if you ever meet. Refer each other to spicy websites in your messages.

💜 Then, when you can't stand the suspense anymore, arrange for a face-to-face meeting.

💜 Spend the evening looking at naughty websites, including stories of erotica and erotic art. Then try out of a few of the things you've learned.

Nice

Behind the Mask

Halloween has become a booming industry. More and more adults are choosing to join their younger counterparts by dressing up. But really, why should you have to wait until October 31st?

❤ Attend a masquerade ball with your mate. Select costumes that reflect the theme of the event. Have fun and dress as a famous duo, such as Antony and Cleopatra or Laurel and Hardy. In addition to being a good time, many of these events raise money for worthy charities.

❤ On Halloween, get in touch with your inner child and go trick-or-treating. Spend the afternoon together recreating favorite costumes. At sundown, roam the streets begging for candy. As an alternative, stay home and greet the neighborhood kids as they come looking for goodies.

❤ For a laugh, pass some time in a local costume shop with your partner. Become a grand Victorian lady or a knight from King Arthur's round table, if only for a few minutes.

Naughty

Tricks and Treats

Do you long to dress in costume but find the usual hobo or ghost options lacking something? Be adventurous and plan an evening that appeals to more adult tastes.

- ❤ Host a "Pimp and Prostitute" party. Turn your home into a raucous bordello for the evening. Indicate that yours is a house of ill repute with a red light out front. Ask your guests to dress the part.
- ❤ Upon arrival, give each couple $1000 in play money. Throughout the evening, the pimps should try to strike deals with the other guests for their clients' services. The guests with the most money at the end of the party win.
- ❤ For something more intimate, create an evening of cinematic romance by dressing as lovers from the silver screen. Valentino, Zorro, Mae West, and Marilyn Monroe are all characters that could heat things up. With a little help from both the leading players, this movie is sure to be rated "for mature audiences only."

Nice

Love Is in the Air

Spring brings a sense of renewal to our lives. Bright green leaves unfurl from buds, and flowers open their pastel petals in the gentle sun.

❤ Take to the outdoors and enjoy spring in your own way. Visit a botanical garden or a flower show. Head to your local garden store or nursery and pick up some colorful plants to add spring to your home, both indoors and outdoors. Plant them in your yard or in windowboxes.

❤ Have a picnic in your backyard or a nearby park. Take a festive kite and fly it while your partner takes a nap on the blanket. Buy small grapevine wreaths, dried flowers, and ribbons and make your own medieval headpieces, or make Easter bonnets from paper plates like you did in school!

❤ Attend an outdoor concert or take a weekend trip to watch a spring training baseball game.

spring fling

Naughty

Spring Fever
Welcome spring into your home by making your bedroom a love nest.

- ❤ Arrange floral-scented potpourri or candles around the room. Get roses from a florist that are past their prime, pull off all the petals, and sprinkle them onto the bedsheets. Put on floral-printed robes or nightwear. With the spring movement of Vivaldi's *Four Seasons* playing in the background, make love in your own spring garden.
- ❤ The Maypole is an ancient ritual in which young people danced around a pole holding ribbons that were attached to the top and twisting them around the pole. It was originally a fertility ceremony, with the pole symbolizing the male anatomy, so be warned! Make your own Maypole using soft, silky ribbons however you like. You can even name yourself as King or Queen of the May.
- ❤ A Playboy bunny outfit may be the perfect way to get things hopping!

naughty or nice sex | 127

Nice

Season of Sun

As the days grow longer, thoughts often turn to baseball games and family trips to the shores of the nearest body of water. That's right, summer is here!

💜 Take a day off and spend it with your mate at a local community park. Lounge beneath a shade tree and enjoy a cooler full of thirst-quenching sodas and deli sandwiches. Push each other high into the sky on a swing or take a tandem trip down a slide.

💜 Escape the sun for a while and ask your partner to help you find the perfect pair of sunglasses. On the way home, stop at your favorite ice cream stand and share a cone.

💜 Host a clambake for neighborhood friends. Prepare lots of scrumptious food and homemade lemonade. Challenge your guests to a game of badminton in the backyard.

💜 When the sun sets late in the evening, catch fireflies and set them free.

Naughty

Heat Wave

As children, summer meant freedom from dreary classrooms and mountains of homework. Take the opportunity for a summer escape, just you and your mate.

- ♥ Dare to go bare at a clothing-optional tropical destination. Many all-inclusive resorts offer relaxing accommodations for couples who like to go *au naturel*. Enjoy a sensuous getaway on the beach as you succumb to the nudist within you.

- ♥ If you and your lover prefer to stay closer to home, plan a private day by the pool. Shop for a tiny string bikini or Speedo bathing suit. Mix a large pitcher of frozen drinks and spend an afternoon in the sun. Make sure to apply plenty of sunscreen.

- ♥ Try staying cool the old-fashioned way. Surround your bed with several fans. Place a tub of ice in front of each fan to create a cool breeze on your skin. Playfully run ice along your mate's body. Temperatures will rise!

naughty or nice sex | 129

Nice

Stayin' Alive

The 1970s had a very definite presence in the fashion, music, and attitudes of the time. Travel back to that decade and catch disco fever.

❤ Go to a thrift store or costume shop and look at 1970s fashions: polyester double-knit shirts, tight long-sleeved sweaters, hip huggers, platform shoes, and wide belts.

❤ Rent the definitive 1970s movie, *Saturday Night Fever*, and dance during the nightclub scenes. For a little extra help, get an instructional video on disco dancing and practice your moves. Then show them off at a dance club that features this music.

❤ Dig out your old disco record albums and cassettes and have a '70s night at home together. Or listen to a radio station that features 1970s music. Have disco-era food like crock-pot chili, buffalo chicken wings, or quiche. Think up clever call signs, or "handles" that you would use for each other if you were talking via CB radios. Ten-four, good buddy!

boogie nights

Naughty

Disco Inferno
Remember mood rings? They contained heat-sensitive stones that purportedly changed color based on your emotions.

❤ Be a human mood ring during your next sexual encounter. As you're warming up in your love-making, call out these colors to let your mate know how your mood is progressing: brown means I'm waiting, green means I'm warming up, blue means you've got my attention, purple means I'm warm, and red means I'm hot.

❤ For the big '70s adventure, rent a Chevy van with a tape player, drive to the woods, and make it rock while your favorite disco music is blaring. Make a sign for the window like the classic bumper sticker: "Don't come knockin' if this van's rockin'."

❤ Have your own Studio 54 at home for the evening—minus the drugs, of course. Wear your sleaziest '70s attire, blast some disco music, and seduce each other on the dance floor.

Nice

And in This Corner

The world of professional wrestling is bold, bad, and colorful. It's big on hype, starting with the wrestlers' names. Those monikers tell the audience and the opponents what they're in for.

- Watch professional wrestling at home, live, or at a sports bar, read some magazines about it, and think about why the wrestlers chose their particular names.
- Now, make up your own professional wrestler names for you and your partner. Take advantage of your attributes, nicknames you've had in the past, words that rhyme with your first or last names, or physical characteristics. Beef it up with an idea of what your strengths would be in the ring.
- Watch Olympic wrestling on TV or attend a high school or college wrestling match.
- For another kind of contact sport, take boxing or kickboxing lessons together. Practice sparring at the gym or get a punching bag for home. Can you go nine rounds?

Naughty

Are You Ready to Rumble?

Professional wrestlers know how to play up their images by capitalizing on their ominous names, tough talk, and form-fitting uniforms.

- ♥ Once you have your professional wrestler name picked, prepare your image. Get black leotards or Spandex outfits. Black is the preferred, get-down-to-business color. Decorate your costumes with glitter or felt details like flames, fringe, and chains.

- ♥ Next, fix your hair big with hair spray and even spray-on hair color in neon colors. Get some face paints from a novelty shop and do your makeup, as fierce-looking or as sexy-looking as you dare. Slap on some fake tattoos and a clip-on ring on your eyebrow, nose, or belly button.

- ♥ If you're bold enough, attend a wrestling match this way, or at least watch one on TV in costume. Choose different wrestlers to root for and cheer them on ferociously.

- ♥ If you're really fans, your rivalry will probably erupt into at least an arm-wrestling match and possibly a full body-contact wrestling match. You'll both end up down for the count.

Nice

Looking for Love

Have you ever thought about how you would describe yourself in a personal ad? Do this fun activity with your partner.

❤ Sit down together and browse through the personals section of your local newspaper. Venture into a "Just for Fun" or "Other" category and have fun trying to decipher the cryptic acronyms.

❤ Now get paper and pencil or use the computer to write personal ads about yourselves. You can be factual or exaggerate wildly. Now exchange them and see if you agree with each others' descriptions. Then write personal ads about each other, making them complimentary and even boastful about your partner's wonderful qualities.

❤ As a surprise for a birthday or anniversary, write a personal ad that declares your love for your mate (using nicknames) and send it to the local newspaper for the personal ad section.

Naughty

It Pays to Advertise

Let's face it. Personal ads are supposed to "sell" the person on their attributes, whether they're real or imagined!

❤ Using the personal ads from a newspaper, cut and paste together a sexy description of yourself. Have your mate do the same. Exchange your ads and see if there is any truth in advertising.

❤ Next, write personal ads about yourselves that describe you as very sexual beings. You can be realistic or fantastic in your details. Make the descriptions irresistible.

❤ Then write them about each other, building the person up as a super sexpot. Comment on how your mate does in the way of performance, satisfaction, and service. Exchange them and read them out loud to each other in your best bedroom voices. You'll probably want to verify the accuracy of these claims!

Nice

Transparent Treasures

Why not take some time out with your mate to explore the old adage that what you see is what you get?

💜 Spend an afternoon window-shopping with your partner. Stroll down your local antique row or wander through a multilevel mall. Seek out unique shops that you may have otherwise overlooked. Don't step foot in a store, just enjoy the creatively assembled window displays.

💜 Take a glass-bottom boat tour and experience the wonders that lie just below the water's surface. Visit a local aquarium and learn more about the mysteries of the sea.

💜 Surprise your mate with a small token of your affection. Wrap the gift in festive colored cellophane or a decorative clear plastic box.

💜 Tour a local church or cathedral and marvel at the beauty of the stained-glass windows. Later, if you're feeling crafty, try making your own stained-glass keepsake.

crystal clear

Naughty

Sheer Delight
Seeing may be believing, but almost seeing can be divine torture! Plan an evening to drive your mate to distraction.

❤ Go shopping together for the latest in barely there fashion. Indulge in a delicate see-through teddy or sexy mesh briefs to turn your lover's head. Many adult clothing stores and catalogs cater to those with a taste for the exotic.

❤ Create a racy ensemble to welcome your partner home. Cover your body in clear plastic wrap or bubble wrap used for packing fragile items. Instruct your mate to open with care.

❤ Stage your own private wet T-shirt contest. Shower with your mate wearing only a white T-shirt and white cotton panties or boxers shorts. Allow the fabric to become transparent as the water splashes over your bodies.

❤ Make love on a sheet of heavy clear plastic. Use a touch of scented massage oil to reduce sticking and you'll slide away to ecstasy.

Nice

Puttering Around

Golf combines all the great elements of recreation: being out-doors, playing a sport, spending time with friends, and celebrating at the end.

- 💜 Play nine or eighteen holes of golf at a local course, or get away to a resort for a weekend or an entire week of fun on the green. To enhance your game, take a lesson together. You can also travel to a professional tournament and be part of the crowd. Quiet, please.
- 💜 Miniature golf is a fun way to practice putting in a colorful, themed environment. Watch out for the windmills.
- 💜 For indoor fun, spend the afternoon together watching golf on TV, play a golf video game, watch an instructional video, read a golf magazine, or buy an indoor practice putting green or a children's toy golf set. Fore!

Naughty

Tee for Two
Dimples aren't only found on golf balls. Does your partner have any? There's only one way to find out.

❤ Once you've learned the basic golf swing from a lesson or a how-to video tape, practice together in the nude! Set up a putting green on a flat surface and hit the ball into a cup. Now, take turns being the instructor. Stand close behind your partner with your arms atop your mate's arms on the golf club. Practice the backswing and the forward swing over and over until you get a rhythm going. See where it takes you.

❤ Since you have your own private staff, take a shower with your caddy and then give each other rubdowns after your strenuous practice.

❤ Celebrate your love-making with golf-themed chocolates or a swig of scotch from Scotland, the home of golf.

Nice

Jumpin' Jive
All you cool cats and crazy kittens, grab your partners and cut a rug because swing is king!

- 💜 Make a beeline to your local video store and rent a movie to get you and your mate "in the mood." Selections like *Swing Kids* or *Swingers* are sure to get your blood pumping and your feet tapping.
- 💜 Afraid you have two left feet? Enroll yourself and your partner in weekly dance lessons. Before long you'll be jitter-bugging like old pros.
- 💜 Step out with your baby for a night on the town. Go to a swing club or attend a big band charity dance. Dress to impress in clothes from the period. Talk your mate into entering the dance contest.
- 💜 If you're not quite ready to unleash your moves on an unsuspecting world, move the furniture aside and create a dance floor in the living room. Stir up a couple of cocktails and get ready to jump, jive, and wail!

swing time

Naughty

Dirty Boogie

Ever fantasized about a chance encounter with an attractive stranger in a dimly lit lounge? Fantasize no more, because the Kit Kat Club is open for business.

- ♥ Plan a swinging evening for yourself and your mate. Create a sultry atmosphere on your patio or in your living room with a small table draped with a deep red cloth.
- ♥ Complete the setting with a small candle and a card that reads "Reserved for Lovers."
- ♥ Turn the lights down low and play some of your favorite music from the '40s. Pretend you're a lonely cigarette girl just finishing your shift or a GI in town on leave, looking for a friendly face.

- ♥ Offer your mate a drink from the bar or share a slow dance together. As the hour grows late, retire to your room for a nightcap and a bit of hanky panky!

Nice

Sleigh Bells Ring
Let it snow! When the cold North wind begins to blow, bundle up and enjoy the frostiness together doing outdoor activities.

❤ Spend the day or weekend going sledding, coaster-riding, or tobogganing. Riding together nestled on the same sled is one sure way to stay warm! Then build a snowman, or make two snow people that look like the two of you. At night, go ice skating, which is especially romantic in front of a bonfire. Be sure to toast marshmallows. When you get home, warm your rosy cheeks by the fire and give each other foot massages to warm up those toes.

❤ Take off for a getaway at a winter resort that offers downhill or cross-country skiing. If you don't know how, take lessons. Rent a snowmobile and head into the woods. Settle in for a nostalgic sleigh ride, then snuggle by the fireplace in the lodge or in your own room sipping hot tea or cider. Soak together in a steamy hot tub.

As We Dream by the Fire

Turn up the heat on your relationship this winter by creating a warm love nest for just the two of you.

- If you're home, snuggle together under an electric blanket. Heat massage oil in a dish of warm water and then lovingly rub each other down. Burn pine or balsam candles or incense to give your bedroom the aroma of a rustic alpine cabin.
- Or take a romantic trip to the mountains of Colorado or Switzerland to enjoy the snow-covered beauty. Ski together or learn snowboarding. Go on a tour of a brewery and sample some beers. Then in the evening, enjoy hot toddies in front of the fireplace.
- Get your own private hot tub or sneak into the resort's public spa at midnight and make love in the soothing water. Then lie together on a bearskin rug in front of the fireplace or in the loft covered in plaid wool blankets.

Nice

Lock Down

Do the schedules that you and your mate keep leave little time to just relax? Close your organizer and hide the car keys, you're under house arrest!

💜 Choose a day when you and your partner are not allowed to leave the house. You'll both be surprised at all you can find to do. Spend the day playing cards or piecing together a jigsaw puzzle. If you're feeling ambitious, tackle a household project that has been nagging at you.

💜 Make a game of seeing how many things you can do from the comfort of your own home. Today's technology affords you the luxury of doing many things without stepping foot out of the house. Call for take-out, watch a home-shopping program, or browse the Internet together looking for bargains.

💜 Plan a prison-themed movie festival. Spend the day watching movies like *The Birdman of Alcatraz*, *The Shawshank Redemption*, and *Stir Crazy*. Solitary confinement is much more enjoyable when spent with the one you love!

Naughty

Passion Parole

Do you have the feeling that you and your mate have been on the lam from love? It may be time to issue an erotic arrest warrant.

❤ Plan to spend some time incarcerated in the sensual slammer. Visit an adult novelty store and purchase a pair of handcuffs or other exciting restraints. Many of these stores feature specialty cuffs lined in soft faux fur.

❤ Treat your mate to an evening as a prisoner of love. With your partner's permission, make a citizen's arrest. Gently cuff and lead your lover into the bedroom for a prolonged strip search. Be sure to handle any concealed weapons with care.

❤ As this naughty prison's warden, you'll be responsible for the well-being of your inmate. Come up with creative ways

to make your lover's term more tolerable. Some "exercise" in the yard may be just what's needed. By the end of the evening, your mate will be begging for an extended sentence!

Nice

Everybody, Let's Rock
We're gonna rock around the clock tonight. Take a musical trip back in time to the bobby-soxers era.

- 💜 Don your finest 1950s outfits from head to toe. For men, that means slicking back your hair and wearing a button-down shirt, trousers, and penny loafers. If you have a varsity letter sweater, perfect! Women, wear a ponytail (whether your own or one courtesy of a beauty supply store), a starched white blouse, poodle skirt, white ankle socks, and saddle shoes.

- 💜 Head for a burger place that has outdoor seating or drive-up service. Enjoy a creamy malted, ice cream soda, or milkshake. Play 1950s music in the car. Then put the windows down, turn the music up, and cruise the circuit, chewing bubble gum. Head for a '50s dance club and rock 'til broad daylight.

- 💜 Then take a day or weekend trip to a classic car show, perhaps in a city you've never explored before.

Naughty

Two Silhouettes on the Shade

In the '50s, the bad boys wore jeans, white T-shirts, and black leather jackets. Decide whether you and your mate are going to be good or bad for the evening. Maybe it's more fun to each pick a different angle.

- ♥ Buy Coke in classic glass bottles, grab a bowl of popcorn, and go in the basement to watch TV. Lie on the floor together. Let those Roman hands and Russian fingers take you wherever you want to go. Play spin the bottle.

- ♥ Now you're ready to rent a cherry red or turquoise 1957 Chevy and cruise the town on a Saturday night. If you can't find one of the vanishing drive-in movie theaters, park at a scenic lookout or a secluded area. Get in the back seat and make out. How far will you go on the first date? What's your curfew?

- ♥ Get a class ring and present it to your partner. Do you agree to go steady? What does that mean?

Nice

Groovy Times

The '60s were a time of newfound freedom. Folk music, long hair and bell-bottoms dominated the scene. Plan some time to get in touch with your inner flower child.

- ❤ Get a taste of the Woodstock experience by attending an outdoor music festival. In the summer months, many music groups band together to offer traveling concerts. Spend a day lost in music with the one you love.

- ❤ Tap into your social consciousness. Ask your mate to get involved with you in a cause you both feel strongly about. Information on social and environment groups can be found on the Internet. Attend a peaceful demonstration or volunteer your time to help the less fortunate.

- ❤ You don't have to be a hippie to dress like one. Tie-dye T-shirts together. Choose bright colored dye and use string or rubber bands to create wild patterns on the fabric. You'll be having fun and feeling groovy!

Naughty

Love-In

Rebellious youth shed their inhibitions about sex in the '60s. Free love reigned supreme. Why not continue the trend and start your own sexual revolution?

- ❤ Take a road trip in a vintage VW van. Set out with no particular destination in mind. Let the wind be your guide. Stop frequently to make love. It's the only way to travel.
- ❤ Shed your everyday worries and clothes with a visit to a nudist's resort. Travel to a nearby clothing-optional beach.

Liberate your body and spirit by spending time together in the all-together.

- ❤ Ladies, join your '60s counterparts and ban the bra. Guys can join in by outlawing underwear. Choose an entire day to go without any undergarments.
- ❤ Cancel any plans you may have for the weekend and stage a love-in with your mate. Tune out everyday distractions and spend the weekend making love. Far out, man!

Nice

The Riches of Asia

Asia features a wealth of different cultures and the wisdom of thousands of years. Discover some of the secrets these lands have to offer.

❤ Feast on a type of Asian cuisine you've never had, such as Thai, Chinese, Japanese, Vietnamese, Malaysian, or Indonesian.

❤ Buy fortune cookies and remove the fortunes carefully. Then sit down with your mate and write new ones that tell how you feel about each other. Insert them carefully into the cookies and exchange them. Enjoy them with Japanese tea served in small round cups.

❤ Study the Chinese art of feng shui, where the placement of objects in the environment affects the flow of energy. You can do this for your bedroom, the whole house, or your office.

❤ For some active fun, take a martial arts class together. There are many to choose from: tae kwon do, karate, jujit-su, and tai chi. When you get done, you may have to register your hands as lethal weapons!

Naughty

The Smiling Geisha

The geisha, or Japanese courtesan, is a figure of great mystery. Going back to ancient times, geishas are schooled in providing pleasure. They know exactly what their partner wants. Do you?

- ❤ You or your mate, or both, can dress up like geishas. (You've seen *Madame Butterfly?*) Wear bright colored silk robes and platform shoes or sandals. Now, use costume grease pencils to make your face very white, your lips very red, and your eyes heavily lined with black.

- ❤ Hang a wind chime in the bedroom and run a fan on it to create mystical far Eastern sounds. Light sandalwood incense sticks or cones.

- ❤ Have a meal of sushi seated on cushions around a low table or a makeshift table from a cardboard box or ottoman. Use chopsticks and serve saké or plum wine.

- ❤ Now take turns being the geisha, pleasuring your partner with singing, dancing, massage, and intriguing sexual acts.

Nice

At Your Service

Wonder what it would be like to have a personal assistant who caters to your every whim? Schedule a day with your mate to share a taste of the good life.

💜 Draw straws or flip a coin to decide who will be the first to be waited on. As the servant, spend your time going out of your way for your mate.

💜 Prepare a lavish meal, run a warm bath, or wash the car for your partner. Halfway through the day, switch places and get ready to be pampered.

💜 At the end of the day, treat each other to a peppermint foot massage and laugh about the day's events.

💜 As an alternative, you and your mate can each make a small list of chores that need to be done. Trade lists and spend the day in your loved one's shoes. You'll gain a new perspective on all that your mate does.

Naughty

Sensual Servitude

Imagine coming home after a long week of work to find someone who will do anything you ask! Stop dreaming and set aside a weekend for you and your lover to become sexual slaves.

💜 Start by each choosing a racy outfit for the other to wear. Try taking a walk on the wild side and purchase a leather collar or other accessory from an adult boutique.

💜 Choose who will be the first to serve and spend the evening making your master's fantasies come true. The following evening switch roles. Remember to play nice.

💜 Create a book of love coupons together. Make each coupon worth a romantic encounter. "One session of extended foreplay" or "Passionate sex on the patio" are perfect ideas. Divide the coupons equally and redeem at your own risk!

Nice

Peanuts and Cracker Jack

Take me out to the ball game! Baseball's great whether you watch it at home, attend a game at a nearby stadium, or take a weekend trip to see your favorite team at an away game.

♥ Settle in for a Saturday afternoon or a weeknight baseball game. Wear your team jerseys and hats. Have hot dogs and your favorite beverages. Or rent a video about a sports legend, one of the greatest games of all time, or funny moments in sports history.

♥ Then head for a weekend sports card show and see what valuable trading cards you now have or remember owning as a child.

♥ If it's not baseball season, attend a football game, an Olympics event, a bowling tournament, or a tennis match. Have a pick-up game of basketball at the local court, or attend an amateur sporting event such as a Little League baseball game. It's not whether you win or lose, it's how you play the game.

Naughty

Give Me an L-O-V-E

Cheerleaders add a certain spice to sporting events and have a reputation to match.

💜 Dress up in your skimpiest, tightest cheerleader attire and do a cheer specifically designed for your mate. Rent a silly or sexy cheerleading movie.

💜 Spend the weekend at a sports-themed resort, where you can participate in sports together or separately. Some feature a particular sport such as tennis or golf. After your lessons, treat yourself to a soothing massage and a healthy meal. There's nothing like working up a sweat to give you an appetite…for each other.

💜 When you're watching a baseball game in your hotel or at home, determine with your mate what it means "to get to first base," second base, third base, and a home run in your sexual vocabulary. As you're watching the game, when a batter gets to first base, go there! Let's hope it's a high-scoring game.

Nice

Merry Christmas, Darling
The holidays are the season for celebrating with time-honored traditions at home. Share some of those, just the two of you.

- ❤ Talk about the holiday traditions you each enjoyed as a child. What was special about that time for you?
- ❤ Spend an afternoon baking Christmas treats together. Make a gingerbread house that is modeled after your current home or another building of significance.
- ❤ Have your picture taken together and put it on a Christmas card, or make your own card using the computer. For a festive postmark, send your prestamped cards to the postmaster in Christmas, Florida, North Pole, New York, or Santa Claus, Indiana. (Check the Internet for the current zip codes.)
- ❤ Spread holiday cheer by calling or emailing family and friends you haven't talked to in a while. When you curl up together with some warm cider, wassail, or wine, and listen to Christmas carols, your troubles will be miles away.

deck the halls

Ho, Ho, Ho

You'd better watch out, because Santa knows who has been bad and who has been good. However, sometimes being bad can be fun.

- ❤ Get your own Santa Claus or elf costumes at a costume shop or retail store. Sassy elves wear hip boots and tight red Spandex suits. Now take turns being Santa. As you sit on Santa's lap, try your hardest to convince the old elf that you really want those things.

- ❤ Snuggle together under flannel sheets and watch your favorite Christmas movies. Eat cookies and milk in bed.

- ❤ Wrap yourself in Christmas wrapping paper only and stand by the tree when your mate comes home.

- ❤ Just as Santa makes a list, you and your partner can each make a list of the "good" and "bad" things you've done this year. Think about what you can do differently in the year ahead, then forgive yourselves and each other.

- ❤ Plan a winter getaway to a resort that features sleigh rides in the snow, walking in a winter wonderland, and cozy cabins with fireplaces. As the song goes, "All I want for Christmas is you."

Nice

Your Most Romantic Place

What is your idea of paradise: a tropical island, a mountain cottage, or a European city? What is your mate's ideal romantic setting? Take a trip to experience it firsthand, or create the environment right in your home.

- 💜 If it's tropical heat you want, head for the beaches of Miami, the Caribbean, or Bermuda. To bring the tropics to you, create the perfect setting in your home. Crank up the heat (if it's not summer), bring all of your plants into the room, play steel drum music, serve Caribbean food, make rum drinks, and have a limbo contest.
- 💜 If you crave cold, head for the mountains of Washington or New England, or even Austria or Tibet. For times when you can't get away, turn down the temperature, put on sweaters, and have hot chocolate or hot brandy while snuggling under a blanket.
- 💜 Find out what your mate's romantic paradise is and create it as a special birthday surprise.

Naughty

Saturate Your Senses

What's your idea of paradise in the bedroom? What colors, scents, textures, and tastes do you hunger for? Set it up for your mate as a surprise evening or weekend interlude.

- ❤ Is the color black sexy and mysterious to you? Buy naughty black loungewear for yourself and your mate.

- ❤ If you like smooth fabrics against your skin, buy black satin sheets. If you like the puffy softness of velour, buy a rich (but inexpensive) black velour blanket so you can get lost in the sensuous folds. Dye gauze or cheesecloth black and drape the bed in it, tying it to the corner posts with big black velvet bows.

- ❤ Bathe the room in flickering shadows from black, scented candles in your favorite fragrances. Licorice will continue your spicy theme nicely.

- ❤ Now prepare your favorite drinks, perhaps Black Russians and black caviar on crackers. Turn on your favorite music and then your mate!

Nice

Harvest Happiness

As the weather grows cooler and the holidays approach, thoughts turn to family and friends. Why not enjoy all that the fall season has to offer with the one that you love?

❤ Attend a harvest festival with your mate. Sample some of the season's delicacies, like warm pumpkin bread or spiced apple cider. Browse through the crafts created in rich earth tones. Snuggle together around a roaring bonfire.

❤ Travel to the country for a romantic evening hayride. Get lost in the rhythm of the horse's hooves as you and your mate sit among the bales of hay. Marvel at the trees displaying their fall colors.

❤ Visit a pumpkin patch and choose a specimen perfect for carving. Spend the afternoon creating a jack-o-lantern together. Roast the pumpkin seeds for a tasty treat. Any of these activities is sure to warm your hearth and heart!

autumn ardor

Fall for You

During the autumn months, erotic thoughts can wane as bodies are lost beneath layers of warm clothing. Why not shed some of those clothes and turn up the heat?

- ❤ Plan an evening in front of the fire with your mate. Snuggle together wearing nothing but an old bulky sweater or a pair of thermal long johns. Curl up under a blanket and share a bottle of wine. Make love as the fire's embers smolder. Bearskin rug optional.
- ❤ Sink into luxury and spend time together soaking in an outdoor Jacuzzi. When the weather turns cold, a steamy session can really get your blood flowing. The air will be chilly, so be sure to have a pair of thirsty robes on hand.
- ❤ Giving yard work a sexy spin will have you and your mate scrambling to get outdoors. Rake leaves in your backyard into a pile. Jump in and make love in the warmth of the afternoon sun. Nothing like a little lusty landscaping!

Nice

It's Greek to Me

The ancient Greeks lived the good life. They created great works of art and architecture, cultivated grapes, established city-states, and built ships. Take the highlights of this civilization and make a day or a week out of it.

- ♥ Watch a travel video and read a travel guide about Greece, or take a trip there. Or visit a nearby museum that has an exhibit of ancient or modern Greek works.
- ♥ Read up on Greek mythology. Name yourselves after the Greek gods you are most like. For women, your choices include Hera, queen of the gods, Artemis, goddess of the moon and the hunt, and Aphrodite, goddess of love and beauty. For men, there's Zeus, king of the gods, Eros, god of love, and Hercules, god of strength.
- ♥ Attend a Greek festival. Try stuffed grape leaves, lamb or seafood kebabs, moussaka, olives, baklava, and a Greek salad featuring feta cheese. Complete the meal with a nice Greek wine.
- ♥ For a fun evening at home, dress up in bedsheet togas and watch *Odysseus, Zorba the Greek*, or even *Caligula*.

Naughty

Revelry and Ribaldry

Toga, toga! **Turn your living room or bedroom into a raucous ancient Greek festival.**

- Decorate with heaping bowls of grapes and silver goblets of wine. Hang green, leafy garlands around the room and festoon it in white fabric. Burn candles on tall stands. Dine on exotic goat's milk and figs, a known aphrodisiac.
- Now wrap yourselves in togas made from bedsheets and create olive-branch wreaths for your heads using silk garlands from a craft store. Complete the look with sandals.
- The ancient Greeks originated the Olympic games. Thing is, they played in the nude. Develop your own naughty, nude Olympic events. Go for the gold.
- In the Greek legend, Odysseus went on a perilous sea voyage. Among the dangers was passage through waters where the tantalizing Sirens tried to lure sailors to their deaths with their singing. Odysseus had himself bound to the mast to avoid caving in. Tie your partner to the bedpost. Can you make your mate succumb to your charms?

Nice

Switching Seasons

Have you ever found yourself dreaming of the beach on a cold winter day or wishing the heat would break in the middle of the summer? Pick a day when you and your mate can turn the seasons on their head!

❤ If you are missing the flavor of a grilled steak, plan a cookout in the middle of the winter. Make it a real picnic by using paper plates and plastic utensils.

❤ Take a winter stroll on the beach. Layer on your warmest clothing and hold hands as you walk along the shore. Play Frisbee in the snow.

❤ Treat your mate to an escape from the summer sun with a visit to an indoor ice rink. Put on your favorite sweater, lace up your skates, and dazzle your partner with your fancy footwork.

❤ Celebrate Christmas in July with an artificial tree and carols. These ideas will make any season a season of love!

Naughty

Heating It Up

Are you feeling like you and your mate are stuck in a seasonal rut? It may be time to turn up (or down) the heat. Transform your home into a haven from the weather outside.

❤ Schedule some time to drive away those winter blues. Turn up the heat in your house and spend the day wearing the skimpiest swimsuits you own.

❤ Enjoy fruity tropical drinks and spread out your beach towels. Be sure to rub each other down with suntan oil. You don't want to get a nasty burn!

❤ Take a break from the sweltering summer. Crank up the air conditioning and create your own winter wonderland. Build a small, romantic fire in the fireplace.

❤ Sip hot chocolate and snuggle up under a blanket. Make love with your socks on in front of the fire. Now that's a summer vacation!

Nice

You're in My Heart

Valentine's Day is the most romantic day of the year. Celebrate it by creating your own handmade cards for each other.

- ❤ Take pictures of each other, close-ups so you can see the faces very well. Using the ones of yourself, make a collage or put one in the middle of the card. Now use red and pink construction paper, lace doilies, ribbons, and stickers of Cupid and hearts to dress it up. Finish it by writing on it a loving declaration of your feelings.

- ❤ Or buy a box of children's Valentine's Day cards, such as cartoon characters, super heroes, or a toy. Sign all of them to your mate, using different messages.

- ❤ Order a pizza with the pepperoni arranged in the shape of a heart, or pack your partner's lunch with favorite foods.

- ❤ With a bouquet of daisies, do the classic "He/She loves me, loves me not," but use the words "I love you because…" for each petal.

be my valentine

Naughty

As Naked as Cupid
The tradition of sending Valentine cards probably comes from a pagan ritual in honor of the goddess Juno. Start your own rituals using the naughty side of your personality.

- ♥ Buy some special Valentine's Day lingerie, such as red silk boxer shorts or robe, skimpy red lace panties, or a long, red negligee with elbow-length gloves, which feel very sexy when run across bare skin. Visit a novelty store and buy naughty chocolates or edible underwear.
- ♥ Slip into red satin sheets, illuminate the room with spice-scented candles, and feed each other gourmet chocolates in bed. Play your favorite romantic or sexy music.
- ♥ Get temporary tattoos of hearts or Cupids and put them on each other.
- ♥ Or take on the role of Cupid, wearing only a pair of wings and a halo and holding a toy bow and arrow. Try to get your partner under your spell. For maximum cherubic effect, paint your body with red or gold body paints or glitter.

Nice

Laugh Lines
Sometimes life has a way of getting a little too serious. Why not take some time out with your mate to enjoy the lighter side of life?

❤ Watch your favorite comedy with the one you love. Whether you enjoy the bawdy humor of *Animal House* or the rapid-fire banter of Tracy and Hepburn, sharing it with your mate is sure to bring a smile to both your faces.

❤ Enjoy an evening out at a local comedy club. Pick a venue that features a stand-up comedian or improvisational group. If you or your mate would like to get in on the act, find a club with an "open mic" night.

❤ Spend an afternoon sharing your favorite childhood jokes. Be sure to laugh at the bad ones! Take a hint from *Candid Camera* and plan a light-hearted practical joke on a friend together. Laugh and the world laughs with you.

Naughty

Dirty Jokesters

Have you ever been at the height of passion and suddenly burst out laughing? Okay, that may not be appropriate, but these ideas will have you and your lover laughing all the way to the bedroom!

- ❤ A little competition is always healthy in a love relationship. Start a tickling competition with your mate. Rolling around, laughing on the sofa can make even the nightly news a little lighter. The one who gives up first owes the winner a massage.
- ❤ Snuggle up in bed and share a book of dirty jokes. They may not be politically correct, but these jokes can be very funny. Are they giving you any ideas?
- ❤ Act out your favorite "farmer's daughter" joke. It seems like there was always an endless parade of traveling salesmen and wayward travelers stopping at the farmer's house. Solve the mystery and find out what the farmer's daughter really had to offer!

Nice

Tender Loving Care

Does your mate like to be pampered when feeling under the weather? Who doesn't? The next time your partner gets a little scrape or a minor ailment, offer him or her some extra-special treatment!

💜 Give your mate several get-well cards, stick on colorful children's Band-Aid bandages even if they aren't necessary, buy flowers, stock the house with favorite comfort foods and cook them as requested, have the patient take fun children's vitamins, and call several times a day to check on progress.

💜 If you can stay home from work for a day just to be there, put on a white doctor's coat or nurse's outfit and frequently take your partner's pulse and temperature. Get a comfy quilt, plenty of glasses of water or juice, and be sure to plump the pillows frequently.

💜 For an extra-special treat, arrange for a singing telegram or a massage therapist to come by. All of this special treatment is bound to speed the healing.

Sexual Healing

So you're not a doctor, and you don't play one on TV. But we've all played the game as children. Dust off those phony credentials and slip on the scrubs.

❤ Suit up in a white lab coat or white nurse's dress, or order real surgical scrubs from a catalog or online service. They come in many different colors and prints.

❤ Now, one of you can play the patient by wearing nothing but a few feet of paper towels (you know how comfortable those paper clothes are!) and lying down on the bed. Have the other come into the room—knocking first, of course—wearing the doctor coat. Do the usual checks of knee reflexes, heart rate, and all-over body exam. Then, using a natural sponge and a dish of water, do a little pre-op washing all over.

❤ Or play out the scenario you've seen on those medical TV shows, where two medical professionals get hot and heavy in a supply room or another forbidden area of the hospital. Quick, someone could open the door!

Nice

Play by the Rules

Rules, rules, rules! They are everywhere. School, work, and relationships all come with their own sets of rules. Not all rules have to be restricting. Why not create some rules you won't mind following?

❤ With your mate, decide on a rule that the two of you must follow for an entire day. Create a "Compliment Your Mate" or "Love Note" day. Put your heads together and come up with an idea for each day of the week.

❤ Visit a toy store and purchase a new board game. Instead of reading and following the instructions, make up your own rules. Or create your own game based on your relationship.

❤ Spend an evening talking with your mate honestly about the rules of your relationship. If there are issues you don't agree on, discuss what compromises can be made. Remember, the two of you share control of this set of rules.

Naughty

Breaking the Rules

Are you and your lover rebels? Do you go out of your way to break the rules? If not, it could be time to throw caution to the wind.

💜 Do you and your mate avoid public displays of affection? This could be because of rules you learned while still in school. Make today the day to break those rules!

💜 Go to the movies and make out in the back row of the theater. Slip your shoes off and play footsie under the table at dinner. Spend the afternoon shopping and make out in a dressing room.

💜 Play a game of "Rules" over the weekend. Choose some guidelines to make your time together more romantic. Set a rule that you can't talk about work, or that clothing can't be worn in the bedroom. When one of you breaks a rule, the other gets to choose an appropriate punishment. Be fair but firm!

Nice

Once upon a Time

The land of fairy tales grows farther away as we get older. What's your favorite story? Your mate's? Take a trip back in time and indulge yourself and your mate by recreating your favorite fairy tale at home.

- ❤ If it's *Cinderella*, take a carriage ride and then go ballroom dancing. "Lose" one of your shoes as you leave the dance floor. (Oh, and be sure to be home by midnight.)
- ❤ If it's *Snow White* or *Sleeping Beauty*, head for the forest on horseback and reenact the scene where the Prince awakens her with a kiss.
- ❤ If it's *Hansel and Gretel*, go for a walk in the woods, but make it a happy ending by taking a picnic lunch with gingerbread cookies—and a compass.
- ❤ If it's *The Princess and the Pea*, put a special gift under your partner's side of the mattress. Ask in the morning if it was discovered. Surprise! Chances are, your mate's not a prince or princess, but you probably knew that anyway.

Naughty

Spellbound

The original Grimm Brothers fairy tales were harsher than the Disney versions we see today. Give these stories a naughty twist by doing your own bedroom versions of the classic tales.

💜 If *Beauty and the Beast* is your favorite, take on these roles, with one of you being gruff and the other trying to soothe the savage beast.

💜 If you love *The Little Mermaid*, get in the bathtub and see if your mate can break the spell that cost you your voice.

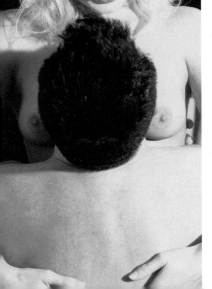

💜 Then there's Pinocchio with his growing nose. Come on, use your imagination.

💜 Perhaps the lord in *Rumpelstiltskin* can be talked out of locking you in the attic with the right persuasion. You can even have props such as straw and gold, so that you can appear to be meeting his wishes.

💜 In *Little Red Riding Hood*, the Wolf can probably be talked out of eating you, but will most likely be hungry for something.

Nice

Welcome Home

Everyone enjoys celebrating special events. Weddings, graduations, and anniversaries are only a few of the occasions that call for festive gatherings. Don't limit yourself to only these big events. Every day is cause for a celebration!

❤ Does it seem like your mate has been out of town on business for weeks? Welcome your loved one home in style.

❤ Plan a surprise gathering with your partner's closest friends and family. Create a "Welcome Home" banner that everyone can personalize with handwritten messages. Decorate with colorful streamers and balloons. Serve all of your partner's favorite foods. Greet your mate with a cheer of "Surprise!"

❤ For a more intimate celebration, choose a night during the week to welcome your mate back from the workday. Flowers, wine, and a candlelit dinner are a great way to show how much you care.

Naughty

Home Bodies

If your love life is taking a backseat to business meetings and deadlines, it's time to rediscover that home is where the heart is!

- Pick a day to leave the office early and meet your partner at home. Have a bottle of wine chilling and uncork it as the two of you work together to create a favorite meal.
- Set the table with your best china and linens. Enhance the mood with romantic music and lower the lights. Don't talk about work over dinner. Discuss current events, movies, or a book you have read.
- After you have helped each other clear the dishes, enjoy a soak in the bathtub. Lather up and gently wash each other.
- Towel dry and head into the bedroom. Treat your lover to an extended round of foreplay. When you think you can't wait any longer, make love late into the night. There's no place like home!

Nice

More Than Granola

Health food stores offer a variety of food and personal care products that will enrich your life.

- ♥ Go to a store together and pick out items you've never experienced, along with things you would normally eat. Be daring! Get the ingredients for a meal and cook it together.
- ♥ Spend the whole day eating healthy, including lots of your favorite produce. Make fruit smoothies in the blender or old-fashioned, fresh-squeezed lemonade.
- ♥ Then go out for some exercise of your favorite kind. Take a stretching or yoga class together and then practice at home.
- ♥ Attend a health fair to sample new products or go to a New Age fair or festival. Check out the aromatherapy, herbal oils, and crystals.
- ♥ For fun at home, cook up your own soap using glycerin and other natural ingredients. Or buy herbs, dry them, and put them in a bottle of warmed olive oil so that they make a flavorful oil for dipping bread later on.

Naughty

Feels Natural

Being limber in the bedroom will open up a world of possibilities. Get the most out of life by stretching those muscles.

- ❤ Get a book or videotape on stretching, yoga, and other exercises that couples can do together. Try them first clothed, then strip down and do them together naked.
- ❤ Set out aromatherapy oils, candles, or incense, and create a healing environment. Play soft instrumental or New Age music. Run a fan on wind chimes, or get a Tibetan prayer bowl and enact its soothing hum.
- ❤ Buy some soaps, salt or sugar scrubs, and a loofah at the health food store and try them out in the shower or tub.
- ❤ Now break out the lotions and oils. Put a thick towel on your bed to create your own massage table. Watch a video tape or refer to a book on massage and practice the moves on each other. Tell your partner where it hurts. You can also get a seaweed wrap or mud pack for deep cleaning and refreshment.

Nice

Creations in Clay

Do you and your mate long to find an outlet for your artistic inclinations? Try taking a tip from the great sculptors of the Renaissance. Roll up your sleeves and get your hands dirty!

❤ Investigate class offerings at the local community college or art institute. Sign up to take a class that interests you both. Choose a life form sculpting or pottery class.

❤ For a unique night out, visit a "paint your own pottery" gallery. These stores are popping up in many areas. For a small fee, you and your partner can choose from a variety of ceramics to bring to life. Many of these venues offer food and beverages in addition to art supplies.

❤ Give the game of charades a creative twist by acting the clues out using modeling clay. Invite some friends over and form two teams. You don't need to be Michelangelo to appreciate this laugh-filled gathering!

Mold and Model

Who would have thought that working with clay could be so sexy? Demi Moore and Patrick Swayze immortalized the passion of pottery in the movie *Ghost*.

💜 Recreate this famous love scene with your mate. Borrow or rent a portable pottery wheel for the evening. Dim the lights and play The Righteous Brothers' "Unchained Melody" softly in the background. Add some clay and water and let your imagination do the rest. Be sure to spread out an old sheet or plastic drop cloth. Things could get messy!

💜 Practice sculpting the human form with your lover as the model. Ask your mate to pose nude for you. Create the perfect pose by gently moving your lover's body. Linger over your partner's skin.

💜 Knead your mate's muscles like clay. Encourage your lover to return the favor and give each other a deep body massage. Who needs clay to create a masterpiece?

kissing tag

Nice

Pucker Up

Remember the game of tag? All the kids ran around like crazy, and the one who was "it" had to tag someone else, who would then be "it." Spice up the concept by turning it into kissing tag.

💜 If you do this at home, go about your normal activities. Each time you pass each other, share a kiss.

💜 Or, if you need some extra cash, do the carnival game of selling kisses. Set up a booth, perhaps a cardboard box on top of the dining room or kitchen table, and tell your mate that each kiss can be purchased for a dollar. What will you do with all that money?

💜 When you go out together to do errands, go to a big store and split up. Each time you spy each other, exchange a kiss. Or play the game of "it" and chase each other, discreetly, of course, through the grocery store, kissing when you're caught. Tag, you're it!

kissing tag

Naughty

Sticker Shock

Take the game of tag indoors, using the entire house for your playing field. This time, instead of using kisses to designate who's it, use stickers, and play naked.

❤ First, strip down and do some warm-up stretches. Now, break out some stickers, postage-stamp size or bigger, and designate a home base. To determine who will be "it," roll a pair of dice. Take off running through your place, slapping your mate with as many stickers in as many silly places as possible. Each time one of you gets to home base, the other is it.

❤ You can also add the element of hide and seek, by taking turns hiding. When you find your mate, plaster on as many stickers as you can before your partner gets to home base.

❤ After ten minutes, call time and count up how many stickers you have each been tagged with. Then slowly pull them off and give each other rub-downs to cool off after all that activity. You'll both be winners in this game.

Nice

Generous Genies

Wouldn't it be wonderful to have your very own personal genie? All your wildest dreams granted with just the rub of a bottle. Get out your polishing cloth and let the rubbing begin!

- ❤ Create a genie bottle to be used by you and your mate. Make it shimmer with plastic jewels and rhinestones. Write your fondest wishes on slips of paper and place them in the bottle.
- ❤ When you have a day to spend together, open your genie bottle and choose a wish to grant. You may have to get creative if the wish is a large one. "I wish for a new car" can be granted by spending the afternoon browsing through a new car lot.
- ❤ Put your heads together and come up with a list of three wishes that the two of you agree on. Use your bottle to collect loose change and extra money toward fulfilling your wish. Your wish is the genie's command!

Naughty

Arabian Nights

Do tales of Aladdin and his magic lamp leave you wishing for romantic adventures in a faraway locale? Say "open sesame" and unlock the passion of a hot Arabian night!

- 💜 Turn your home into an exotic palace fit for a prince or princess. Have soothing sitar music drifting throughout the house. The flickering light from oil lamps adds an air of romance.

- 💜 Create a royal bedchamber by enshrouding your bed in soft, billowing fabric. Outfit the bed in sensuous satin sheets and burn fragrant incense to lend to the atmosphere.

- 💜 Greet your master at the door dressed in genie attire. Sheer fabrics are best for highlighting your wish-granting abilities. Treat your lover to a magic carpet ride. Any throw rug will work nicely. Hold on tight as you make love and send your mate soaring through the clouds!

Nice

Fat Tuesday

The wild spectacle of Mardi Gras in New Orleans has become an annual event for many partygoers each February. If braving the crowds isn't your style, make plans to celebrate at home with your mate.

- Throw a celebration for family and friends. Decorate your home with festive purple, green, and gold decorations and create some of your own Mardi Gras traditions.
- Work in the kitchen with your mate to bake a king cake for the occasion. King cakes contain a plastic baby that represents the baby Jesus.
- The person finding the baby is said to have good luck for the following year. That person is also responsible for making the cake the next year.
- String beads and make feathery masks to hand out to your guests as party favors. Serve spicy Cajun dishes to add just the right amount of heat to your gathering!

party gras

Naughty

Beads and Baubles

On Fat Tuesday, revelers in New Orleans are treated to a parade that features scantily clad dancers perched atop large floats. The sexy tradition of flashing intimate body parts for a string of beads has also become part of the craziness.

❤ Attend a local Mardi Gras celebration with your mate. Design sexy, revealing costumes to wear that reflect the occasion. Tiny gold shorts, skintight tops, and feathered headdresses are perfect choices. Be sure to arm yourself with enough strands of beads to last through an entire night of adventure.

❤ Plan an erotic Mardi Gras event for just you and your lover. Using body paints, decorate each other with brightly colored designs. Linger over your mate's intimate areas while creating a human work of art.

❤ With an armload of beads ready, prompt your lover to dance and flash you in return for a strand of beads. Start a competition to see who ends up with all the beads at the end of the evening!

Nice

Easy Riders

Motorcycles have long represented freedom and a sense of daring. Cycling aficionados are of all ages and come from all walks of life. It is their shared love of the open road that brings them together.

💜 Rent or borrow a motorcycle and treat your mate to an afternoon tooling around the countryside. Feel the bike come alive beneath you as you explore the back roads of your area together.

💜 Attend a local bike rally with other motorcycle enthusiasts. Often the proceeds go to benefit a local charity.

💜 Plan a vacation with your partner to attend the annual Bike Week in Daytona Beach, Florida. Meet new friends and browse the latest in motorcycle accessories.

💜 Even if you don't own a bike, dress like you do. Go shopping for a pair of biking boots or leather pants. You'll both be looking like cool riders!

Naughty

Sexy Cycles

Aside from being incredibly liberating, motorcycles carry with them a certain sense of sexual freedom. When else are you urged to put something exciting between your legs?

❤ Attend a motorcycle festival and wear the skimpiest clothing you own. Bikers are not ashamed to show off their bodies, and for good reason. The ladies often sport sexy halter-tops and cut-off shorts, while the men wear skintight jeans and show off their bare chests.

❤ Enter a "Sexiest Biker" competition. These events allow you to strut your stuff in front of a more-than-appreciative crowd. Give a knowing wink as your mate watches from the audience.

❤ Plan a seductive motorcycle rendezvous for yourself and your lover in your garage. Put down the kickstand and take off your clothes. Make love right there on the seat. Detailing a bike has never been this fun!

Nice

Proud to Be an American

Let your patriotism show by taking a day, weekend, or week-long trip to a site of historical significance. Make it your own tribute to the United States!

❤ Go to an event such as a parade, concert, memorial service, or movie that celebrates a patriotic holiday, such as Memorial Day, the Fourth of July, Veterans Day, Armistice Day, or D-Day. Take a picnic lunch and snuggle as the fireworks burst above your heads. Talk about which of our fifty states you have visited while you share an apple pie you baked together.

❤ Visit a place of historical significance, such as Boston, Philadelphia, The Alamo, or Washington, D.C. If you're nature lovers, experience the beauty of a national park.

❤ Volunteer to support a cause that's important to both of you. Perhaps it's campaigning for a political candidate, working the polls on election day, building a house for charity, or taking part in a community event such as a landscape beautification project. You'll be making the world a better place.

Naughty

Oh, Say Can You See

How deep does your patriotism run? Are you red, white, and blue all over? Let your mate find out.

- Before you head out to a patriotic event, put red, white, or blue star stickers all over your body. You can also apply a flag-shaped temporary tattoo to your cheek or make one yourself with face paints. Or conceal it somewhere on your body and tell your mate about it when you get to the event, or about the patriotic underwear you're wearing.

- Hide fifty stars all over your body—some covered by clothing, some not. When you get home, tell your mate to find all fifty. Then make your own fireworks.

- Buy a board game or card game based on trivia about the fifty nifty United States, the presidents, or other patriotic history. For every answer you get wrong, you have to remove an article of clothing.

- Sexy versions of Uncle Sam costumes are available at party or novelty stores, as are star-studded uniforms like the ones the Dallas Cowboy cheerleaders wear. Remember, Uncle Sam wants you!

Nice

Seeing Green

Do you and your mate enjoy all the festivities surrounding St. Patrick's Day? Why wait until March 17th? Enjoy a little of the Emerald Isle any day of the year!

💜 Pack a picnic lunch and head out to a meadow in search of four-leaf clovers. Although not easy to find, four-leaf clovers are considered very lucky.

💜 Spend the afternoon creating the perfect green beer. Add green food coloring to your favorite ale. As an alternative, visit a pub and enjoy a beer while listening to some traditional Irish music.

💜 Attend a St. Patrick's Day parade or festival. Everyone becomes a little Irish at these events. Hone your accent by speaking to each other with a brogue all day.

💜 Experiment with some traditional Irish dishes in the kitchen. Make corned beef and cabbage or bangers and mash. These should satisfy the leprechaun in anyone!

luck o' the irish

Lusty Leprechauns

In Irish folklore, leprechauns are known as devilish little sprites that always have a trick up their sleeves. Take a tip from these tiny rascals and treat your mate to some mischief with an Irish flair!

❤ Without your lover knowing, apply a temporary shamrock tattoo somewhere on your body. Be creative and pick an intimate area where it won't easily be discovered.

❤ Lead your mate on a sexy search for the coveted four-leaf clover. Inform your partner of all the riches that will come to the person finding this magical charm. Your lover won't believe the luck.

❤ Create two small pots of gold coins like those desired by leprechauns. Spend the evening coming up with seductive ways to swindle each other out of your treasures.

❤ Barter for sexual favors using your allotted coins. But is the winner the one who collects the most money? No matter, you'll both be over the rainbow!

Nice

Good PR

As soulmates, you and your partner are each other's staunchest supporters. Put your feelings into words by becoming each other's public relations agents.

❤ Sit down together with a stopwatch or a watch with a second counter and write thirty-second radio commercials that tell how wonderful your mate is. "Sell" your partner by using descriptive words and your most enthusiastic tone. Then read them to each other in your best radio announcer voices.

❤ Now, write a short press release that describes your partner's great qualities. Pretend you're introducing your mate to the world. Explain what makes your partner so appealing.

❤ You can also write a newspaper announcement about your partner's accomplishments, perhaps a new job or promotion, or an award. Some towns will publish these blurbs in the local paper.

❤ For a birthday gift, videotape your mate's friends and family members extolling all of his or her wonderful qualities. Have them include funny stories that illustrate these points. Invite them over for the video's premiere.

Naughty

Tabloid Journalism

The headlines of the supermarket tabloids reveal all kinds of personal information about celebrities' exploits. They often include intimate details about their sex lives. Can you compete? Start your own sex-capades and put them on paper.

💜 Write a steamy review of your mate's best sexual performance. Add a lot of detail, including some that didn't happen! Make it read like a scene from an erotic movie or a steamy novel.

💜 For one week, keep journals about the scorching thoughts you have about each other when you're not together. Then, on Saturday night, read the week's entries to each other. It's bound to spark some excitement.

💜 Or find the steamy part of a novel or play, read it to each other, then act it out. You can also watch a racy scene from a movie and do the same.

💜 Celebrities do crazy things, like making love in the back of a limousine, during a party at someone else's house, on a rooftop, or in a pool. What's your fantasy? Live it!

Nice

On the High Seas

When the sun reaches its apex high in the sky and balmy breezes kiss your skin, thoughts often turn to cool, refreshing water. Grab your mate and make a beeline for the nearest river, lake, or ocean.

- Pack up the tackle box and head out for a deep-sea fishing adventure. Book a charter and go after the legendary "one that got away."
- If you're looking for something faster-paced, rent a boat and go water-skiing. Release the Big Kahuna within and treat your partner to a day of surfing.
- Can't make it to the ocean this weekend? Sign the two of you up for scuba diving lessons. Many areas offer beginning lessons. Once you've been certified, plan a diving trip to an exotic location.
- Schedule a trip to the Florida Keys and snorkel among the bright tropical fish and pristine reefs. Whatever you choose will make a big splash!

on the water

Naughty

Love Boat

There's nothing quite like romance on the open water. The gentle roll of the waves lulling you into a relaxed state, sultry winds heating up the nights, and your lover held close as you watch the stars twinkling on the water. Jump on board, it's full speed ahead!

- 💜 Plan a weekend getaway to the Bahamas. Many cruise lines offer three-day packages that make stops in Nassau and their own private islands.

- 💜 Spend your days napping together in the sun or taking a chance in the shipboard casino. Better yet, put up the "Do Not Disturb" sign and make love the entire trip.

- 💜 Borrow or rent a boat and enjoy a day basking in the sun. If the boat has a cabin, go below deck for an intimate encounter. The combination of your sensual motion and the rocking of the boat is sure to make your lover wish you could be stranded together on a deserted island.

Nice

Today Is Your Birthday

What's your partner's favorite way to celebrate a birthday? Just the two of you together, with family members or a few close friends, or with a crowd? Does your mate like surprises or not?

❤ Find out and plan the perfect evening. This may require talking with friends and family members and doing some spy-like questioning of your partner.

❤ If your partner likes surprises, go to a favorite restaurant or for a weekend trip to a favorite place, such as a fishing camp or resort town.

❤ If your mate would rather help plan the event, pick a theme so that everyone can come in costume or with a certain type of gift. The theme could be sports, favorite TV shows or movies, or an evening playing cards or classic board games.

❤ Or, pick a special location for meeting friends and family, such as a sports bar, video arcade, hotel lounge, miniature golf course, skating rink, or movie theater. Many restaurants create special moments for birthdays, so be sure to tell the manager.

another candle

Naughty

Birthday Suits

Even someone who doesn't like surprises will like these birth-day festivities, because they take place in the privacy of your own home.

❤ When your mate comes in from work on the big day, wear only wrapping paper and a big bow on top of your head. Stick a big tag on yourself that says, "Surprise inside" or your own naughty message. Let the paper fly.

❤ Bring the birthday cake into the bedroom. After the candles are out, feed each other cake. Then dab each other with the icing and lick it off.

❤ Or make a giant "cake" out of a very large cardboard box or a smaller one stacked atop a larger one. Paint them white and decorate them with colored streamers and bows. When your partner arrives home, pop out of it wearing nothing but a smile.

❤ A guy or girl can do a sexy rendition of the birthday song, à la Marilyn Monroe. Or have a singing telegram courier or sexy stripper-gram messenger deliver the message. This will light your fires for your own private birthday celebration!

Nice

Keeping Pace

Although life flies by at such a quick pace, our society can't seem to get enough of things that go fast. Buckle up, shift into gear, and away you go!

💜 Challenge your mate to a couple laps at the local go-cart track. Some areas even offer attractions that simulate drag racing. Or visit an amusement park and have a smashing time on the bumper cars.

💜 If you and your mate are feeling lucky, visit a track and play the ponies (or puppies). Limit yourself to $20 spending money and cheer on your favorites in the trifecta.

💜 Join a running club and train for a 5K race together. Running is a great way to get into shape and have fun at the same time.

💜 NASCAR has become one of the fastest growing sports in the United States. Make plans to attend or watch an event on television. You'll find yourself in the winner's circle!

Naughty

Start Your Engines

Ever since its introduction, we have had an endless fascination with the automobile. Race cars hold a special place in the hearts of daredevils of all ages. These ideas are sure to have your lover purring like a kitten!

💜 Rent or borrow a sports car for the day. After spending some time exploring the open road, find a nice secluded place to park. Make out in the back seat like a couple of teenagers out past curfew.

💜 Spend a sunny afternoon washing and waxing your car. The combination of soapsuds and a tight white T-shirt and cut-off shorts should get your lover all revved up. Things may get so hot that you'll have to hose each other down.

💜 As an alternative to cars, take part in a naked foot race. Several nudist communities offer events run in the all-together. Lace up your shoes and let it all hang out!

Nice

Ring in the New

As the last sands of the old year slip through the hourglass, spend some time with old acquaintances. They won't soon be forgotten!

❤ Break out your best party dress or tuxedo to welcome in the new year at a black-tie affair. Pull out all the stops and hire a limousine to chauffeur you and your mate on a night of dinner and dancing.

❤ Make plans to spend the holiday at the heart of all the New Year's festivities, Times Square. Book your trip early and reserve a hotel room that overlooks the bustling crowd.

❤ Looking for something a bit more relaxed? Usher in the new year snuggled on the couch with the one you love. Prepare favorite appetizers and share a bottle of champagne as you celebrate the passing of another year in several different time zones.

❤ Host a holiday fireworks display in your backyard. You'll be starting off the new year with a real BANG!

Naughty

All That Glitters

Are you expecting a shiny new year? Plan a special New Year's Eve that's sure to put a gleam in your lover's eye.

💜 Spend the holiday at home with your mate wearing little other than a strategically placed party hat or pair of sequin pasties with tassels. A touch of gold body glitter should add the right amount of shimmer to the evening. There'll be no need for noisemakers as you make your own sensual noise.

💜 Decide on an unusually daring place to make love for the first time in the new year. The anticipation will make those final minutes seem like hours. As the clock strikes twelve, head out for your risqué rendezvous.

💜 Create a list of sexual resolutions to keep in the new year. Share your secret yearnings and make promises that will bring you both pleasure. When the countdown ends, the fun begins. Looks like it's going to be a very good year!

naughty or nice sex | 203

about the authors

Amy Scott and Boyd Geary are writers living in Orlando, Florida. They began writing together while working for a frontrunner in the entertainment and amusement industry. Boyd designs and delivers training courses and seminars, and Amy designs multimedia presentations and programs.